Winning Mr. Wrong

Winning Mr. Wrong

MARIE HIGGINS

WALNUT SPRINGS PRESS

To my wonderful husband, Scott, for having faith in me.

Walnut Springs Press, LLC
110 South 800 West
Brigham City, Utah 84302
http://walnutspringspress.blogspot.com

Copyright © 2010 by Marie Higgins

ISBN: 978-1-935217-76-3

Acknowledgements

First, I would like to thank my wonderful critique partner, Melissa Blue, for brainstorming with me and talking to me for hours on the phone. You're the greatest. Thanks to my critique group, who helped me correct glaring errors and taught me a few things about writing, and to Amy and Gail, for helping me fine-tune the Christian aspects of *Winning Mr. Wrong*. Also, I am grateful to my beautiful and supportive daughters, Chrystal, Heather, and Shea, for always accepting the fact that their mother is a romance writer, and for laughing with me as we read parts of this story together. And lastly, a big thank you to Walnut Springs Press, who believed in me, and to Linda Prince Mulleneaux, for liking my story enough to read it within a week.

Chapter One ♡

Charlene Randall drove her fiery red Honda into the covered parking space, killed the engine, and yanked the keys out of the ignition.

Tonight would be the one-month anniversary of her breakup with Tim, and she wished she had forgotten about it. Never again would he come over after work with his purebred toy poodle, who always yapped in a high pitch and threatened to tear off her big toe.

Okay, so Charley wouldn't really miss Jaws as much as she would miss the tangy scent of Tim's aftershave. Too bad she liked his scent more than she liked him. Even now she couldn't quite remember the shade of his eyes.

Yet thinking about having a man in her life weighed deeply in her heart, and she wished it didn't. It was her fault loneliness invaded her life right now. That truth was hard to swallow.

She snagged her leather briefcase from the passenger's seat, stuffed with material she'd have to look over before the next morning's meeting with Sacramento's Channel Nine directors, and climbed out of the car. Another evening keeping company with news reports rather than a man! She sighed. People had said, *Charley, life will go on.* But she had seen little evidence besides the fact that the sun still rose and set—and she was still very much alone.

Oh, she'd said her daily and nightly prayers, asking the Lord to make the ache in her heart disappear. It hadn't. She still wanted someone to talk to, watch television with, or take her out to dinner once in a while.

She grabbed her purse and bumped the car door closed with her hip. Her two-inch heels clicked against the concrete as she hurried toward her townhouse. She fished around in her purse for the remote hooked to her keys. She'd just had the keys in her hand, and the same magical force that eats socks from the dryer had worked again, sucking the keys to the bottom of her Gucci bag. Finally, her fingers brushed over the key chain and she withdrew the remote, aimed it over her shoulder, and clicked the doors locked.

A gentle evening breeze teased the strands of hair that had fallen out of her ponytail and tickled her neck. In an automatic reaction, she flipped a stray lock. It was a good thing she didn't wear her hair long. She already wasted enough time styling it.

Next to her townhouse, shadows danced under the streetlights and throaty giggles floated in the breeze. A movement from the Porsche parked in front of her neighbor's townhouse caught her attention. She recognized the wave of the man's raven hair and the shape of his muscular shoulders.

Damien Giovanni, her single, Italian neighbor who had turned romancing women into a career, was obviously doing what he did best—getting another woman to fall for his charms. Charley rolled her eyes.

On tiptoe, she sneaked toward her front door, not wanting to make her presence known. Damien's deep laughter rang through the quiet night, and Charley paused before reaching her porch. Could his date be over so early in the evening? That man entertained women late into the night just about every night. She didn't want to know what they did. In fact, she wouldn't blame the Lord if He launched a lightning bolt down on Damien just to wake him up and put him on the straight and narrow.

The glow from the streetlight shone upon the figures leaning against each other beside the door of Damien's sports car. Despite herself, Charley angled to get a better look. They looked like two worms in electric-shock therapy. *How disgusting!*

The woman in Damien's arms was his usual five-foot eight, blonde Barbie doll. He laughed again, and the baritone ring sent warm shivers down Charley's spine. She cursed her weakness, admitting she enjoyed hearing his laugh. It always sounded like he knew a secret. Regardless, she couldn't stand men like him who never could settle on one woman.

The Barbie wannabe raked her extra-long, fake fingernails through his hair and linked her arms around his neck. Damien grabbed her closer and planted a kiss on her mouth. Charley grumbled under her breath. Couldn't he do *that* in his house? It was bad enough to hear his voice, but to see him in action . . .

Before she could look away, Damien pushed the woman from him and grinned. "See you later."

Barbie waggled her fingers. "Call me."

"Why? You have my number."

Charley pursed her lips. *The arrogant man.* It didn't matter, though. Women still flocked to him like dieters to a chocolate factory, and they devoured his charm just as quickly.

She clutched the briefcase to her chest and tried to make it to her front door before he spotted her. Damien would certainly know she had witnessed the quaint scene a few seconds ago, and he would never let her live it down. Her neighbor always enjoyed making snide remarks just to rile her—and it worked.

Fumbling with her keys, Charley hurried to find the one that opened her front door. But the keys slipped from her fingers and hit the porch, clanging loudly enough to wake the dead. She scolded her clumsiness, knelt on one knee, and swept her hand over the concrete, searching for them in the dark. Why hadn't she turned on the porch light before she left for work?

"Do you need any help, mi amore?"

She jumped and fell back on her rear. The beating of her heart thundered in her ears, and she placed a hand on her chest. "Damien Giovanni, why do you always sneak up on me like that?"

He bent and grasped her upper arm with one hand and her keys with the other. "Because I like the way you jump."

She yanked her arm away. "One of these days you're going to scare me so bad I'll use my pepper spray on you."

Damien's chest shook with laughter. "Honey, if you're as steady with the little can of pepper spray as you are with your keys, I don't see that as a threat."

Charley gasped and punched his arm, but a grin tugged at her mouth. "Just give me back my keys."

He stepped away and folded his arms. "Say the magic words." He raised his eyebrows in that self-assured, infuriating way of his.

"Emergency 9-1-1?"

He tilted his head and laughed harder. The half moon illuminated his handsome features—straight nose, strong chin, and lips that looked like they'd be heaven to kiss . . . for other women, of course.

"Oh, mi amore, you really know how to tickle my funny bone." He dangled the keys in front of her.

"Yeah, well, you really know how to . . . um . . . irritate me."

She grabbed her keys and turned to unlock the door before he noticed the smile she couldn't hold back.

He leaned against the doorframe. She didn't dare meet his gaze directly, knowing what she'd witnessed between him and his date. There was no reason she should feel any kind of attraction toward him. He was *not* the kind of man who would attend church with her every Sunday, and she highly doubted his top priority was temple marriage.

If Damien were anything but the player she knew him to be, she might have given him a chance when, several months before, he'd first suggested they go on a date. But Charley didn't want one-night stands, and she was tired of the love-'em-and-leave-'em kind of guys. After enduring several broken relationships, she wanted something that lasted. Something better. At age thirty, it was time she got married and had a family.

"I've noticed Tim doesn't come around anymore. Did you two break up?"

Charley lifted one shoulder in a shrug. "Our timing was off, that's all."

"Are you okay?"

"I'm fine."

"You sure?"

She tightened her fingers around the handle of her briefcase. "I'm continuing with my life, just as he's done. I don't see why you're so interested."

Damien held up his hands. "Hey, no need to get upset. You know, one of these days you're going to thank me for being such a nosey neighbor."

She lifted her gaze to his and shook her head. "Only in your dreams, buddy."

He grinned and then stroked her cheek with his finger. "My dear Charlene Randall, someday I will be in your dreams." With a wink, he turned and walked away.

She pushed the door open and rushed inside her townhouse, breathing a sigh of relief. That man made her uncomfortable in more ways than one.

She walked to the bedroom, kicked off her heels, and slid each foot into a fuzzy purple slipper. On the nightstand, the picture of her latest flame captured her attention. Actually, *slapped* her face was more like it. Tim's grin used to make her sigh, but now she wanted to spit at the silver-framed 4 by 6.

How dare that man sponge off her for three months, having her pay his bills, buy his groceries, and help him with rent, then leave her for a woman who made more money? And to top it off, he acted like the breakup was Charley's fault. How dare he act like he didn't have to find a job and like all he had to do was keep the sofa warm?

She grabbed the photo, flung it in the small wastebasket a few feet away, and brushed her hands together. *There, that took care of one problem.*

Charley entered the kitchen and took a TV dinner from the freezer—her usual gourmet meal on nights like this. After pulling the meal out of the box and setting it to cook in the microwave, she turned to yet another order of business: collecting information on the Internet for tomorrow's news.

She made herself comfortable on the gray swivel chair and turned on the computer. Whistling a made-up tune, she tapped her fingers on the desktop and waited for the machine to boot. Within minutes, she'd logged onto the Internet. The homepage popped up and she scanned the headlines, searching for something of interest. In the top right of the screen, an article grabbed her attention: "Ten Ways to Win Your Man."

Her explosive laugh disintegrated to a snort. *Yeah, right. Win a man? And there is a certain way to do it? Ha!*

She ignored the link and searched through several other articles, but her mind kept going back. What would it hurt to read it? She had a few minutes until dinner, and she needed a good laugh. She clicked on the hyperlink.

> *What do men find romantic? With the help of Jason Stewart, founder of guyswithemotions.com, we've uncovered just how women can win men's hearts. Below, panelists answer women's questions and bare their souls.*

Charley leaned back in her chair, threading her fingers together over her stomach, eager to read more.

> *1. Dark Chocolates. "Milk chocolate is for kids. Dark chocolate is for falling in love." The chemical Phenethylamine, found in dark chocolate, mimics the feeling you have when you're in love.*

She arched an eyebrow. Very interesting.

> *2. Hard-to-find gifts. A gift that requires effort is sure to be a big hit with the guys.*

> *3. Compliments. The quickest route to a man's heart is through his ego.*

Charley snickered and shook her head.

4. *A night on the town. Take your man on an old-fashioned date. Fix him dinner or go dancing. While in his arms, stare into his eyes.*

5. *Tall buildings. In general, guys like big things. Find a place with a good view. Kiss him under the stars.*

6. *Funny movies. When you can laugh together, you're really connecting.*

7. *Offer to mend his clothes. Believe it or not, most men are old fashioned and love it when a woman can do domestic duties like this.*

8. *Surprise intimacy. Men like it when women surprise them with spontaneous activities on a date.*

9. *Great memories. When you're together, make it memorable. Create memories by taking photos or writing in a journal.*

10. *Tell him 'I love you' in a note. Leave little notes around the house, his office, in his car. Telling him you love him will strengthen the relationship.*

With a sigh, Charley folded her arms across her chest. She'd never done *any* of those things for the men she'd dated. Could that be why she'd never kept them?

The beeping of the microwave jarred her from her thoughts. She pushed away from her computer desk and hurried into the kitchen.

Could this article be a sign? It wouldn't hurt to try it, Charley decided. But who would be her target?

Damien's face popped into her head. She scowled, wishing she hadn't thought of him. He wasn't the kind of man who would get involved in a serious relationship. The last thing she needed was to give her heart to him and have him trade her in for a newer version of Barbie. He would never live up to her moral standards anyway.

She rubbed her forehead and crossed her neighbor off her mental list. So who would be her guinea pig?

The aroma of fried chicken wafted through the air, making her stomach growl. For tonight, she'd put off her experiment and concentrate on filling her stomach.

Tomorrow she'd find a man, and with any luck, she'd make the relationship last.

Close your trap and wipe the drool off your chin.

Charley snapped her mouth shut, hoping she didn't look like a wide-mouth bass as she eyed the handsome blond man walking beside her boss. Fred Murray, Channel Nine's station director, escorted Tall, Brawny, and Gorgeous down the hall, making introductions as they passed offices and cubicles.

The new guy looked familiar, but Charley couldn't recall where she'd seen him before. She jumped from her chair and hurried toward her supervisor's cubicle. Just as she expected, Amanda's curious eyes followed the pair. Charley said a silent prayer of thanks that Amanda was married or her flirty friend would have first dibs.

Charley stopped beside Amanda. "What's so interesting?" Although Charley knew, she didn't want Amanda to think she did.

A knowing smile stretched across Amanda's face. "That's the new guy, Maxwell Harrington. He's taking Phillip's place now that he's retired."

Charley's heart raced. This couldn't be happening, not to her. The dream walking with her boss was Charley's high-school crush! Max was the super jock, the super stud, and he had the super personality all the girls flipped over. Especially her. Although he hadn't been in her ward, they'd been in the same stake, and Charley had followed him around Church activities like a lost puppy . . . secretly, of course.

"Are you serious?" She looked at the two men slowly making their way toward Amanda's desk. "He's the new sports anchorman?"

"Sure is."

"Maxwell Harrington," Charley whispered almost reverently. But this man hardly resembled the boy she'd had a mad crush on for three years. Muscles rippled on his tall frame, and his hair seemed blonder than she remembered as it swept perfectly back from his face. The years had turned him into one looker, that's for sure.

If she'd been the least bit forward, Charley would have hurried over to ask if he remembered her. But that wasn't her style, not even back in high school. Wallpaper was more her style—especially the kind that hid behind furniture and potted plants.

Shyness had always been Charley's biggest downfall with men, which was probably another reason her past four boyfriends had moved on to other women. With all of her failed relationships, she'd collected enough material to write a new best seller called *Breaking Up for Dummies.*

The closer Fred and Maxwell Harrington came, the harder her heart pounded, until she thought the organ would jump right out of her chest. *Give it up, girl. He's out of your league. And if he remembers you, it'll be a miracle.* Yet, with a man like that parading past her cubicle every day, she knew she would continue fantasizing about the unobtainable.

Amanda nudged Charley's elbow, snapping her out of her thoughts. "Here he comes," she muttered under her breath.

Fred, a potbellied older man with a head full of thick, gray hair, stopped in front of them. "Ladies," he began, his smile so big it showed most of his pricey dentures. "This is our new sports anchorman, Maxwell Harrington."

Amanda pushed her way to the front, her arm stretched out in greeting. "Hi, Maxwell. I'm Amanda Shepherd, executive producer."

A smile spread across his beautiful face. "Please, call me Max."

His deep voice made Charley want to sigh, and familiar tingles ran through her. She moved her gaze from his astonishing eyes to Amanda's hand as he shook it, wishing her hand were touching Max's instead of Amanda's.

"So, Max, what brings you to Channel Nine?" her supervisor asked.

"I've been working at a Chicago station for the past six years, and I thought it was time I came back to my hometown."

Max finally let go of Amanda's hand and turned toward Charley. She opened her mouth to speak, but her tongue seemed to swell and her vocal chords froze. She swallowed and tried to begin again.

"Hello." Her voice squeaked. "I'm Charley Randall."

No spark of remembrance lit his eyes, but she didn't give up hope.

"Nice to meet you, Charley." Max's smile widened, making his eyes twinkle.

Her heart fluttered. He paused as if waiting for her to say something else, but all she could do was stare into his brilliant, sea-blue eyes—eyes a girl could drift away in.

"What do you do at Channel Nine?" he asked.

She focused on the conversation instead of her girlish dreams. "I'm the presearch roducer."

Beside her, Amanda laughed condescendingly. Charley's cheeks grew hot, and the dread in her stomach sank lower than the *Titanic*.

She cleared her throat. "I mean, I'm the research producer. I'm Amanda's assistant."

Max's lips twitched as if he held back a laugh. "Well, I hope we'll work together soon."

As Fred and Max continued down the hall, Charley released a mouthful of air. Why did she act so tongue-tied around good-looking men? After her mind returned to normal she realized he didn't remember her at all, and a dull ache formed in her chest. Then again, why would he remember her? They'd never really talked in high school, and certainly not at Church youth activities. She was always the shy and clumsy girl who followed the jocks around like a rock-star groupie. Back then, boys like Max didn't have time to look at unpopular girls like Charley.

When he turned down another hallway out of her view, deep disappointment washed over her. "Wow. He's one fine-looking man."

"Yeah." Amanda squeezed her arm. "And you know all the available women at the station will be after him."

Charley frowned. "So? What does that mean?"

"Well, I would hate for you to get your hopes up."

Charley folded her arms. "Explain yourself."

"You know your track record with men isn't the best." Amanda shrugged. "It's common knowledge."

"Common knowledge for whom?"

"The whole office knows you can't keep a man longer than a couple of months, Charley. In fact, wasn't Tim the longest?"

"Are you saying you don't think I have a chance with Max?"

A sorrowful expression clouded Amanda's eyes. "Well . . ."

Charley flipped her hand through the air. "Don't say it. I know what you're thinking, but you're wrong. The reason I haven't been able to keep a man for longer than a couple of months is because I choose not to." She lifted her chin. "I was bored with the others. Max is different." Of course it helped that he didn't remember her from school—and because he didn't know about the other men and how she lost them.

Amanda patted her shoulder. "But wouldn't you lose interest in him as you did the others?"

The shield Charley had tried to build around her heart crumbled, but she hid her distress behind a smile. "I don't know, and I won't know until I try."

"Then I wish you all the luck in the world." Amanda turned and sat behind her desk, a look of pity on her face.

Anger surged through Charley and she clamped her hands against her sides. How dare Amanda doubt her ability to hold onto a man! She supposed Amanda meant well. After all, her coworker had observed all of her failed relationships.

Charley turned and stormed back to her desk as her dreams of catching Max started to take shape. As much as she wanted to believe she'd been bored with the other men, the plain and simple truth was they had tired of her. Keeping a man for a long period of time wasn't her forte, but this time she would prove she could catch Mr. Heartthrob. And keep him.

When the others had walked out of her life, they'd never really explained why. Wasn't she adventurous enough, spontaneous enough? She had always given in and participated in the activities her dates enjoyed, even when she had no interest in them. Did men get annoyed with her clumsy ways as she tripped over herself to please them?

Max was different. He didn't remember her from school, and he certainly didn't know the woman she was now. She could show him a better side of her personality than she'd shown before. She'd prove to her coworkers she could keep a man.

That man would be the boy Charley had dreamed of for three years in school. The boy she wrote about in her journal every night, and cried over when he took another girl to the prom. The boy she wore black for when he left to go to college—the one she never thought she'd see again.

Was fate finally being kind to her?

She slid into her chair and swiveled back to the computer. With a long exhale, she pushed a lock of hair from her face and looked at the stack of papers on her desk. *Ugh.*

Just like most mornings, Charley checked her personal email first thing. After all, the small television on her desk wasn't giving her any national news she didn't already know. She adjusted her chair, then gripped her computer mouse and clicked the Internet icon.

Thoughts of the article she'd read the night before lifted her spirits. Should she make Max her target? She rolled her eyes. Her chance at winning him was about as good as her chance at winning ten million dollars from Publisher's Clearinghouse.

She clicked on her inbox. Thirty-one messages. Without even looking, she knew most of them were from her mother. Would she ever stop nagging Charley about finding a man and settling down? Couldn't she at least give her daughter better encouragement than "There are other fish in the sea"? Her mother obviously hadn't been fishing in a while.

Soon, Charley closed out of the email program. For some reason, all she could think about now was that ridiculous internet article.

Out of the corner of her eye, she saw Max stroll into the room that would be his office. Another coworker poked her head inside and made a comment that made him smile. Charley's heart leapt. She'd do anything to see him smile at her that way.

She thought back to the article. Should she give it a try? She couldn't bear the thought of another failed relationship, but with "Ten Ways to Win Your Man" to help her, what could go wrong?

Perhaps this was the Lord's way of telling her to go for it.

Her decision made, Charley smiled wide. Give her a couple of days and she'd figure out something intelligent.

Watch out, Maxwell Harrington. Here I come!

♡Chapter Two

Dark chocolate is for falling in love.

Charley's hands shook as she opened the door to the office building. She balanced a box of See's chocolates on her arm and withdrew her key from the lock. The clock on the wall confirmed she was on schedule—one hour before most of her work team arrived.

She walked into the building and stopped to listen. The night team who ran the early morning news was still there. They were few in number, and nowhere near her desk or Max's office.

Her heels resounded through the building like a cannon in the Sistine Chapel. She cringed and lifted her feet one at a time, sliding off her two-inch heels. After picking up her shoes, she tiptoed down the hall. Laughter in the break room made her jump, but luckily nobody came out.

Another noise caught her attention and she sucked in a breath. *Where is that loud, incessant thumping sound coming from?*

Her ears strained as she listened closer. The noise matched

her heartbeat perfectly. She scowled. Why did her heart have to hammer like a tom-tom?

She peeked around the corner of a wall. The offices appeared empty, lights off and doors closed. She breathed a relieved sigh. Everyone must be in the break room.

With the box of candy clutched in her hands, Charley hurried toward Max's office. Soon, she had turned the doorknob and rushed inside.

He'd been working at the station less than three days now, but the scent of his woodsy cologne hung heavy in the warm air. She stopped in the middle of the room, closed her eyes, and exhaled slowly. *Oh, what a man.*

Shrill laughter floated down the hall and plunged her back into reality. She shook away the dreamy images and set the box of chocolates on the corner of his desk. She pressed the card open to make sure he'd see the message.

Your sweetness makes even chocolates jealous. Signed, *Your Admirer.* No way was she going to sign her real name. It was too soon for him to know what she had planned.

As she stared at the box, she visualized Max's reaction. He would saunter into his office in that confident way of his, dressed to kill in his slacks and a white button-down shirt that stretched across his muscles. When he saw the box, his eyes would widen. He'd snatch the card and read it. A smile would spread across his lips, and his blue eyes would twinkle. He'd open the box and pop a chocolate into his mouth. The dreamy expression on his face would let her know the phenylethylamine was working.

With a sudden feeling of love and longing, Max would stop, turn, and look Charley's way. Their gazes would meet. His fingers would touch his lips as he blew a kiss her way. She'd catch it and hold it against her heart. He'd motion with his head for her to come into his office. She'd obey like a person spellbound, not even feeling her feet touch the ground as she floated to him. The door would close, making their meeting private, and he'd take her in his arms . . .

A loud clank down the hall jolted Charley from her daydream. She rushed out of Max's office and stopped, trying to pinpoint the source of the sound.

She sighed. It was just the old furnace kicking on. But it didn't matter. Time to hurry to her desk before someone came.

Lost in thought, she smacked her nylon-clad toes against the wall. Holding her breath, she hopped around on one foot and clutched her throbbing toe. Tears stung her eyes and she gritted her teeth against the pain.

She placed her foot on the floor and limped back to her desk, scanning the offices on her way. *Phew!* She hadn't been caught.

Once at her desk, she turned on her computer. She wanted to appear as if she'd been working, so she scattered a few papers over the top of her desk.

Within half an hour, her forty-two coworkers arrived, but she waited for one in particular. When Max walked in, the whole room seemed to beam just as it used to do in high school. And just like in yesteryear, people greeted him with waves. He nodded, giving them his ear-to-ear smile. Charley sighed.

He stepped into his office with his can of soda in one hand and his briefcase in the other. She leaned forward on her desk, resting her elbows on top as she stared at him through his office window and waited.

His head turned toward the box as he set his cup and briefcase on his desk. After hanging his coat on the rack in the corner, he moved back to his desk. His gaze dropped to the candy. Charley held her breath. Her hands shook so badly that she clasped them together and held them between her knees.

Max grabbed the card and opened it, then stared at it for a few seconds before turning to look out his office door.

Heat rushed to Charley's cheeks and she shuffled through the papers on her desk, hoping to appear busy. She picked one up as if studying it, peeking over the edge at him.

He didn't look her way, and her heart sank. The dream wouldn't happen the way she'd imagined. Not yet, anyway.

When he sat behind his desk and turned on his computer, she scowled. *Isn't he going to eat a piece of chocolate?* He had to!

Glancing at the clock every five minutes didn't help the hour pass any quicker. Every time Max moved from his computer, Charley's heart quickened in hopes he would eat a piece of chocolate. But he seemed completely uninterested in them.

After a few more hours crept by with her mind everywhere except where it should be, Charley pushed away from her desk. She needed a soda, or anything that would keep her mouth and hands busy.

The clicking of high heels echoed on the floor, and soon Amanda sat on the edge of Charley's desk, crinkling a piece of paper beneath her silk skirt.

A smile stretched across the other woman's face as her long, thin leg thumped against the side of the desk, swinging in an uncalculated rhythm. The incessant noise irritated Charley's already frayed nerves, like fingernails on a chalkboard.

"So, Charley. Have you talked to Max lately?"

Charley scowled. "Lower your voice. I don't want the whole office hearing you."

Amanda's eyes widened. "Why? You are after Max, aren't you?"

"Maybe, maybe not. Why?"

"Just wondered if you wanted my help." Amanda extended her arm directly in front of her and waggled her cherry red manicured nails through the air.

Charley took a deep breath and silently counted to ten. Although it made her happy to know her friend wanted to help, now wasn't the best time. She was still too anxious about Max not eating the chocolate.

"Thanks, Amanda. I'll keep your offer in mind."

Amanda shrugged and slid off the side of the desk. "Let me know if you need me." She turned and slinked around the corner toward her own desk.

For the next several hours, Charley regularly glanced toward Max's desk, but the box of chocolates remained untouched. His hand passed right by them when he reached for his root beer, and she wanted to scream when he didn't pick up a piece and plunk it into his mouth.

By the end of the day, her chest ached with frustration. What was wrong with him? He could at least eat one.

She kept her eyes on him until after the six o'clock evening broadcast, and still he had yet to eat the candy. He gathered his personal items and then stopped to look at the box of chocolates. Charley's heart sped and she caught her breath. He picked up the box and walked out of his office. He scanned the area, and finally his gaze rested on her.

With a big smile, Max headed her way. The closer he came, the hotter her face burned.

"Hey, Charley? Do you like chocolate?"

She swallowed hard. "Um, well, yes."

He set the box on her desk. "You can have these. I'd hate to see them go to waste."

She nodded, opening her mouth to ask him why he didn't eat them, but Frank came up behind Max and clapped him on the shoulder.

"You did a great job on the air, Max."

Max turned and walked away with Frank.

Over his shoulder, he called out his goodbyes, passing the others on his way out the door. Tomorrow was his day off, and Charley would have to wait another day to try one of the other nine ways on him.

In momentary defeat, she grabbed the box of chocolates, her purse, and her briefcase, then left the building. Her bottom lip drooped so low she could have tripped on it.

She didn't even remember driving to her townhouse. The place seemed darker than usual, but she ignored the prickly sensations on the back of her neck as she climbed from the car.

The cool night breeze fanned her face as she turned and walked toward the front door. Holding the box of chocolate under her arm, she dug through her purse to find the keys she'd just had before leaving the car. Suddenly, a crack resounded through the air, and she looked up to see the porch light bulb shattered into tiny pieces.

She jumped back to keep from getting cut. The box of candy and her keys slipped from her hand and hit the ground.

A tree blocked the nearest streetlight, making it almost impossible to see. Charley slid her foot around on the porch. Something jingled next to her shoe, but as she bent to retrieve her keys, a shiver ran up her spine. Somebody stood behind her!

A hand snaked out from behind her and clamped over her mouth. The person shoved her face against the brick wall. Pain shot through her skull and she cried out.

Her body shook and her limbs went weak, useless.

"Listen lady," the man whispered in her ear. "Do as I say and you won't get hurt."

She managed a small nod.

"You stay against the wall just like you are now, and I'm going to reach down and get your purse."

Swallowing hard, she nodded again.

After what seemed like an eternity, he removed his hand, but the pressure from his body remained against her. She peeked over her shoulder, but a black mask hid her attacker's face.

Tears stung her eyes and panic nearly consumed her. She couldn't believe this was happening.

The attacker opened her purse with one hand. She could barely breathe.

"Lady, where's your wallet?" he asked suddenly.

Gathering her courage, Charley raised her foot and slammed it down as hard as she could. Her heel connected with the top of his foot and he stepped back with a yelp. She turned, slipped past him, and yelled for help.

The man caught her arm and yanked hard, and she fell to her hands and knees on the concrete. Pain ripped through her body.

Her attacker growled as he threw her onto her back, but she quickly brought her legs up to kick at him. Then, from the shadows, a new form appeared. Like a scene from a Superman movie, another man flew across the porch and landed on top of her attacker, then pulled him off her. Charley crawled out of the way.

The men rolled, but the larger one pinned her attacker on the grass. Her Superman raised his fist and plowed it into the other man's face. The sound of bones cracking echoed through the air, and Charley cringed, even though it was clearly the bad guy who would be hurting.

Through the breeze, she detected a man's musky cologne. *Damien.*

He looked at her over his shoulder. "Charley, my cell phone is clipped to my waist. Call the police."

Still on her hands and knees, she scrambled to him. Her shaky hands brushed across him until she found the cool plastic of the phone. She clicked it open and managed to push 9-1-1.

When a voice came on the line, Charley let out a ragged

breath. "This is Charley Randall at 4010 Meadows Drive number 6. I've been attacked and my neighbor grabbed the guy. Send someone quick, please."

While the 9-1-1 operator probed for more details, Charley's gaze remained leveled on Damien. The man beneath him struggled, but her neighbor tightened his grip and pushed the other man's head into the ground. Through it all, Damien kept glancing her way, giving her an occasional nod and reassuring wink.

After the police questioned her and Damien, and another squad car hauled the assailant to jail, Charley finally crumbled. Damien gathered her in his strong arms and she rested her head on his chest and cried.

The attacker had asked for her wallet, but Charley knew a mugging could easily turn into much worse, even rape or murder or both. Damien had saved her! Once her sobs ceased, she nibbled on her lip and glanced up at him. Had she been wrong about him? Had he been the good guy all this time and she'd just refused to believe it? Maybe he didn't really sleep with all those women he dated. Maybe he was just lonely and had some morals after all!

He helped her into her townhouse and locked the door. Treating her like a fragile piece of china, he walked her to the couch and helped her sit. Then he knelt in front of her.

"Mi amore." He pushed a lock of hair off her forehead. The softness in his brown eyes made her chest tighten. "Do you want me to fix you some coffee?"

"No, I don't drink coffee."

Damien leaned back, his eyes creased at the edges. "Do you want anything to drink?"

"No, nothing."

"Then what do you want?" His finger trailed down her cheek, wiping away her tears. "Would you like me to stay with you tonight?

I can sleep on the couch just to make sure you're all right."

She gave him a weak smile. "No, thanks, I'll be fine."

"Do you want me to check your house first to see if everything looks safe?"

Emotion tugged at her heart. He was acting just like her Prince Charming would act, at least in her dreams. Then it hit her: Damien was acting so sweet only because of what had happened to her tonight. He was simply being kind because she'd been attacked, and any decent man would've come to her rescue. He would be back to his player self tomorrow.

"Thank you. That's a good idea. Search my house, but when you're done, you can leave. I'll be fine."

Damien squeezed her hands before moving away. On his jeans, Charley noticed scuff marks where he and the other man had rolled on the concrete and grass. His light blue cotton shirt molded to his muscles, bunching with his movements.

Suddenly thirsty, Charley stood and, on unsteady legs, made her way into the kitchen for a glass of water. She could also use a sleeping pill tonight.

She heard Damien walk through her townhouse, stopping at each room. When he bounded down the stairs, she pulled away from the kitchen counter to meet him at the bottom step.

He touched her shoulder and looked at her almost tenderly. "Everything looks good."

She sighed. "Thanks again, Damien. You saved my life." She shrugged. "I don't know how to thank you."

The corner of his mouth lifted in an assured grin. "I'll think of a way tomorrow. Tonight, you get some rest."

She frowned. His brain was already back in one-track mode. Still, she was grateful. "Thanks again, Damien."

He caressed her cheek with his fingertips, then turned and walked out the door.

Maybe Charley should have gone to work, but after the previous night's episode, she felt too frazzled. Besides, it was Max's day off. Good enough reason to stay home and recuperate.

Sleep hadn't come easily even with the sleeping pill. She growled and punched her pillow. The memory of the mugging had kept her awake most of the night. Her attacker had been thrown in jail, but her imagination kept telling her he was still out there, just waiting to pounce on her.

Shivering, Charley pulled the blanket up to her chin. Perhaps she should have accepted Damien's offer to stay on her couch. No, because with such an attractive man in the house, she wouldn't have slept at all, just with the thought of him.

After slipping her legs off the bed, she sat and stretched her arms above her head. The only things she planned on accomplishing this morning were showering, dressing, and eating, though not necessarily in that order.

The morning passed too quickly, and with the catnaps Charley took, the afternoon soon disappeared as well. Suddenly it was seven in the evening.

She plopped on the sofa and curled up in a ball. Somehow, she managed to push the mugging incident aside to think about yesterday at work. Max. What a disaster! Tears gathered in her eyes, and if her throat tightened anymore, she'd have to call the paramedics.

What was wrong with her? Maybe Amanda was right. Maybe Charley couldn't attract the sort of man she wanted.

But this was different, wasn't it? This was *Max*, someone she'd loved when she was a teenager—someone who didn't know about her past failures. So why couldn't she get him to notice her? Sure, she thought of herself as a frog, but even frogs found mates, didn't they?

They did. With other frogs.

Maybe I've just set my sights too high, Charley thought. *What I need to find is a small, green, slimy kind of guy, and then I can live happily ever after—in the swamp.*

She groaned and slumped headfirst into the throw pillow. But just as quickly, she sat up and wiped her eyes. She would not give in to despair! There had to be something she could do.

A quick knock at the front door startled her, and she popped up straight like a jack-in-the-box that'd been wound too tight. Once she could breathe again, she tiptoed hesitantly to the door.

"Who is it?" she called, trying to sound confident.

"Your protective neighbor."

With a heavy sigh Charley opened the door. Damien leaned against the frame, looking like a supermodel. His crooked grin warned her he was up to something.

She gave him a hesitant smile. "Hello, Damien."

"Have you eaten dinner yet?"

"No. Why?"

"Because I ordered Chinese, and you know they always bring too much. It's sitting on my table as we speak. I thought you could help me eat it."

She wanted to turn him down, but her stomach grumbled loudly before she could open her mouth to refuse.

Damien chuckled and glanced at her midsection. "I guess that's a yes."

Charley smiled. "Okay, I'll eat with you, but I have a feeling eating isn't the only thing you have planned tonight."

He held up his hands in surrender. "You have me pegged, mi amore."

She nodded. "You know I'm not interested."

He shook his head. "You have it all wrong. I've thought of a way you could pay me back for helping you last night. I have something to make you relax, yet at the same time it will be enjoyable, and something I'm sure you've never experienced."

She gasped, her hand flying to her throat. "Of all the low-down, inconsiderate—"

He pulled on her arm until her hand dropped from her neck. "It's not what you're thinking. I want to try a new product from work on you. You'll be doing me a big favor."

She crinkled her forehead. "Huh?"

"I work at GIO Products, and we're trying out a new product for women. I want you to be my guinea pig."

"What's the product?"

His brown eyes sparkled and he winked. "It's a surprise. Now come on before the food gets cold."

Damien grasped her elbow and tugged. She knew she should turn him down, but she'd always wanted to see how her neighbor lived, and this was her chance. And although she wasn't sure of his intensions, after the previous night, she knew she was physically safe with him. After all, he had saved her life. If he wanted her to do something she didn't want to do, she would just say no.

♡Chapter Three

Damien held his breath, waiting for Charley's refusal. Since he'd met her six months ago, she'd declined all his invitations. Although he teased her endlessly, he admired her for having morals and wanting a real relationship, not a one-night stand. Still, he loved to flirt with her. She was a very attractive woman, and her hypnotic blue eyes practically made him melt. Plus, the cute way she got all riled up made her irresistible. She could make him laugh no matter what mood he was in, and no other woman had ever done that.

When Charley grabbed her keys and stepped onto the porch beside him, Damien felt his jaw drop. He waited while she locked her door, then he took her arm and silently escorted her to his townhouse next door.

She took two steps into his place and her eyes grew wide.

Perhaps he should have warned her he'd redecorated, but he wanted to see her reaction. Instead of the townhouses' standard tan carpet, Damien's living room floor featured large black-and-white domino-tiled shapes.

She blinked. "Wow. What's this, a museum?"

Damien chuckled and walked ahead of her, motioning for her to move into the living room. Her gaze moved to a red chair with a beige cushion that stood against the wall, its back curved perfectly to fit a human form.

Charley shook her head. "I've never seen furniture like this before, except maybe in a Dr. Seuss book."

"That's called a pelican chair." Damien nodded in the direction of her stare. "Christensen and Legaarct designed it, not Dr. Seuss." He pointed to a cherry wood chair. "And that's a chieftain's chair, made by Hansen and Sorensen."

Charley's gaze rested on the final piece of furniture, a black and white sofa.

"And that's a Ross sofa, companioned with a Ross coffee table. Notice how the brushed stainless-steel legs have wooden toes. The veneered tabletop is also stainless steel and has matching vases."

"Let me guess, Ross made them?"

Damien laughed. "No. Hansen and Sorensen."

She turned to look at him, her mouth twisted into a smirk. "Aw, that was my second guess."

Then Charley turned her gaze to the assortment of potted plants scattered on shelves, and to the large pots sitting in the corners of the room. She arched an eyebrow. "Why do you have so many plants?"

"GIO Products is starting a new line of herbal shampoos and conditioners. I've been studying plants for a while now, and most of these are for testing."

She stood next to his couch, running her fingers along the edge. As much as he'd love to see her sitting on it cuddling with him, the overwhelming scent of dinner beckoned Damien, and he pulled her toward the kitchen.

His brown-and-black dining room set was just as fancy as his living room furniture.

"Did Hansen and Sorensen make this, too?" she asked.

"No. Nanna Ditzel did. This set is a Tobago Café."

She arched her eyebrow. "Hmm, I can see why."

He chuckled, knowing she had never heard of the designers or their furniture lines.

The heavenly aroma of Chinese food hung thick in the air. Her stomach growled and he grinned.

She inhaled and closed her eyes. "Yum. What's the specialty tonight?"

"I hope you like sweet-and-sour chicken and lo-mein noodles. There's also a couple of egg rolls and some fried prawns."

She opened her eyes and stared at him. "Are you serious?"

"Yes, why?"

She shrugged. "Those are my favorites."

His chest swelled. At least they had the same taste in food. "Mine, too."

He moved to the chair and pulled it out. She gaped with wide eyes.

"What?" he asked.

"You . . . you pulled out the chair for me."

"So?"

"So most men don't do that anymore."

He winked. "You'll soon discover I'm not like most men."

Charley tore her gaze away from him, then turned and planted her backside on the chair. She wiggled on the seat.

"Well, what do you think? Is it comfortable?"

"Yes. It's hard to believe, but it is."

He retrieved two plates from a cupboard, and soon he placed a plateful of food in front of her. He wondered if she knew how lovely she looked sitting in his kitchen, ready to share a meal with him. It was as if she was meant to be there. Damien had started having romantic feelings for her a few months ago, but she was never interested. He wanted her to be. But with Charley, he'd have to take it slow. Obviously his charm hadn't won her over yet, so he must find another way.

"So, who's the new man in your life?"

She glared at him. "What makes you think I have a new man in my life?"

He shrugged. "I saw you'd brought home a box of chocolates with you last night. I just assumed—"

"Well, you assumed wrong."

He held up his hands in surrender. "Just trying to make small talk."

She relaxed and smiled at him. "I'm sorry. The truth is, you're not too far off. Although I don't have a man in my life, I am trying to."

He walked back to the counter to fix a plate for himself. "Who's the lucky guy?"

She chuckled. "He was my high school crush. Now we work together. His name is Max Harrington."

Damien stopped his hand midway to the box of sweet-and-sour chicken, his breath catching in his throat. Did she just say the name of the man he'd been trying to forget since college?

He looked at her over his shoulder. "Tall, blond, and built like a quarterback? That Maxwell Harrington?"

"You know him?"

Damien turned back to his task, his fingers tightening around the fork. "We were in college together."

"Well, he doesn't know about my track record with men, so I'm going to try a different way to win him over."

"What way is that?" Damien sat across from Charley and started eating.

She explained how she'd run across an Internet article that told women how to win a man, and while she kept a straight face, Damien couldn't do the same. The corner of his mouth twitched as he tried to hold in a laugh. "So that's what the box of chocolates was for?"

"Yes."

"How did it go?" He twirled his fork in his noodles.

"Not very well."

"What happened?"

"He didn't even open the box," Charley said sadly. "How can he detect my scent if he doesn't get that chemical in his blood? It was like blowing a moose mating horn to a deaf moose."

Damien chuckled. "Perhaps he's not a moose."

She rolled her eyes. "Well, I wish I knew what kind of call he likes, but unfortunately, I don't." She sipped her water. "Then again, maybe I read the article wrong. Maybe it said eat chocolates in the dark instead of eating dark chocolate."

"What if this chemical thing is a hoax and it doesn't work?"

"But what if it does? Besides, I checked it out on the Internet. Apparently, tests have been done that support the theory."

"Maybe Max will eat the candy tomorrow." Just saying his name again made Damien cringe.

"No. He gave them back to me without knowing I'm his admirer."

"Ooh, not good." Damien crinkled his forehead.

"My thoughts exactly."

"Did he give a reason why he didn't eat them?"

"No."

"Then you need to think of another way to get that chemical in his blood."

"You're not telling me anything new, but I don't know what to do." She shoveled a pile of rice on her fork.

Damien scratched the side of his face. He really didn't want to help Charley win Max. No girl deserved such punishment, and Damien didn't deserve to be tortured by watching it happen twice in a lifetime. He couldn't stand the rejection. Women *always* picked blond hair and blue eyes over Damien Giovanni.

Although he didn't want to help Charley, he did enjoy her company. A lot. So maybe if he volunteered to help, she'd allow him into her heart as a friend, and eventually their friendship would grow into more.

They ate in silence. As hard as Damien tried not to think of a way to have Max eat the chocolates, Charley's sad eyes tugged on his heartstrings and he wished he could wipe away her frown. The only way to make her smile would be to help her. Hopefully, Max would show his true colors soon and she'd move on to another man. And Damien would be standing next in line.

Funny he felt this way, knowing what kind of girl she was. Yet lately the girls he'd gone out with were boring. Fake. He wanted something new. He wanted Charley.

"I think I know a way."

Her eyes widened. "Really?"

"Does he still drink a can of soda first thing in the morning?"

"Yes."

"All right, here's what you'll do. When Max leaves his office, sneak in and replace it with chocolate milk. Just pour out the soda and pour the chocolate milk in the can." Damien took a swallow of his water to wash down the annoyance rising inside him. "When he sips his drink, the chemical will enter his body."

"That's a wonderful idea. You're the best." She grasped Damien's hand and squeezed.

He winked. "I know."

"This will work. Oh, thank you."

"Anytime."

"Does this mean you'll help me win Max?"

He stared at her for a several seconds. He didn't really want to help her with Max, but if it meant spending more time with her and watching her eyes light up, he'd do it. He'd also be by her side to make certain Max didn't hurt her.

He nodded and she released a big sigh.

"Can you sneak into his office without being seen after he's put his drink on the desk?" he asked.

"Yes. Every morning there's a meeting for the producers and anchor people. The old sports anchorman was usually in there for about ten minutes. If Max follows the same schedule, I can switch the drinks then."

Damien lifted his water glass. "Then let's toast to a successful day."

She raised her glass, clinking it against his. The sparkle came back into her eyes and he wished it was for him. Why had he offered to help when he should be keeping her away from men like Max? Under the table, he bunched his hand into a fist.

He wanted to tell her the truth about his former friend, but maybe Max had changed since college. Damien would ride it out and see what happened. With any luck, she'd quickly tire of Mr. Sportsman.

"Okay, now that we have dinner out of the way, I have something to try on you." He pushed away from the table and held out his hand to her.

"Try on me?"

He chuckled. "Yes, the new GIO product. Don't you trust me?"

The corner of her mouth lifted but she didn't answer. He took her hand and pulled her out of the kitchen, through the front room and toward his bedroom. He hoped she didn't think he was trying to get fresh with her, because that definitely wasn't his intent. It was his own fault she thought poorly of him, and now it was his goal to change her mind.

Unlike most of the women he dated, Charley hadn't acted impressed with his new furniture. Usually the women asked him about what he did for a living and how much money he made. For some reason, Charley didn't care.

He'd always thought she was one beautiful woman, and when he told her so, she didn't like it. Maybe he'd just flirted too much. But every time he saw her, he wanted to see the fire in her eyes—wanted to make her melt in his arms. So far, that hadn't happened. Not even close.

She became a challenge, and now with Max in the picture, it only made the challenge greater. Over the past six months, he'd seen the men in her life come and go, and he'd noticed the pain in her eyes. He didn't want his old college friend to be the next to break her heart.

When they entered his room, Charley stopped and stared at his large bed. "Is this bed from Scandinavia too?"

"Yes. Hans Sandgren Jakobsen designed it. He calls it Grandlit."

She grimaced. "It doesn't look very comfortable."

"Oh, believe me, it is."

A flush of pink stained her cheeks, and he held back a grin. It wasn't very often he was privileged to get this reaction from her. She usually just bit his head off when he said the wrong things.

She glanced at the few pictures hanging on the walls and walked to them. "So, you like the outdoors? Mountains, streams, waterfalls?"

"Yes."

She threw a skeptical glance over her shoulder. "Didn't figure you were the type."

"And what type is that?"

"The rugged outdoorsman."

He shook his head. To him, a man couldn't consider himself masculine unless he loved the wildness of the great mountains.

"I love the outdoors. I even have a cabin in Colorado where I go during the winter."

"Amazing." She smiled.

He took hold of her arm once again and pulled her into his bathroom. She gingerly ran her fingers over his counter, touching his razors, his shaving cream, and a bottle of cologne. Several GIO-brand hair gels, hairsprays, and combs were organized along the top.

As she stared at the products, Damien wanted to be more up front with her. This wasn't just any old testing they were going to do. He owned the company, and tests like this were important. But thanks to some women like his ex, he bit his tongue and confessed nothing. He was tired of women only seeing him for his fat wallet and his sizable bank account.

He motioned for Charley to sit on the small, black-cushioned stool near the garden tub.

When her behind rested on the seat, her back stiffened and her eyes met his. "What are you going to do to me?"

He picked up a hair dryer and handed it to her. A long rod protruded from the front of the dryer.

"What's this?"

"GIO has come out with a new toy. It's a combination hair dryer and curling iron. I'm trying it on you to see if it works."

She crinkled her brows. "And what if it doesn't work? Will I get a lasting perm?"

Damien tipped back his head and laughed. "It's already been tested for safety, if that's what you're worried about."

"Has it been tested on people or dummies?"

"People."

"Were the people dummies?"

He loved her sense of humor. "No."

"Did their hair still look the same afterward?"

"No. It looked better."

"All right, but I'm warning you—"

"Charley, please trust me."

She rolled her eyes but stayed in place.

He walked behind her, reached over to the wall, and plugged in the cord. "First off, let's get your hair a little damp."

He grabbed the water bottle and sprayed her hair. She raised her hands to block the mist from getting in her eyes. After he finished dampening her hair, he took the new contraption from her and flipped it on.

As he played with her hair, the scent of her fruity shampoo drifted upward. Even a hint of her perfume became noticeable, making him want to close his eyes and inhale deeply.

He smiled. She was nothing like his ex. Charley actually cared about people, and he dreamed of the time she would care deeply about him.

Like most women, she probably figured he'd never settle down, just like good ol' Max Harrington hadn't. Inwardly, Damien growled. Out of the two men, *he* would settle down sooner than Harrington.

Why hadn't Damien concentrated on trying to get Charley to like him? Would it matter to her now since she'd set her sights on Max? She'd been in love with Max since high school. But Damien wouldn't give up. In order to charm her and gain her trust, he would have to become her friend first.

Damien gripped the blow dryer harder. Whether she knew it or not, Charley had been on his mind for quite some time. The way she looked at him when she stepped out of her townhouse, pretending she didn't see him with another woman. The way she turned her cute little nose up as if it didn't bother her, even though her bright cheeks told him differently. Especially those times he could make her laugh.

She'd grown on him, and he liked it. How could he make her feel the same way about him? If she'd been the least bit interested, she would have succumbed to his flirtations. She would have gone out with him by now. Wouldn't she?

His heart sank. Once again, a woman picked Mr. Blond Hair and Blue Eyes. Once again, she picked Max.

Damien's chest ached as he realized he wouldn't be the one to hold her or kiss her. His stomach clenched and so did his fingers in her hair. Charley let out a whimper and he loosened his grip. "Did I hurt you?"

"Just a little. It's okay now." She moved in her seat and relaxed her shoulders.

Damien rubbed his forehead, hoping to relieve the pounding in his skull. Although he didn't want to help Charley win Max, he did want to see her happy.

Would the sportsman really make her happy? Several years ago he and Max had parted enemies, and Damien had wanted revenge. Revenge didn't matter any longer, but saving Charley from another heartache did, and Mr. Sportsman would assume Damien wanted Charley out of vengeance. But Damien had liked her long before he realized she knew Max.

Damien sighed. Because he'd offered to help Charley, he was stuck. But he'd make sure Max didn't use her. If it looked as if his former friend was up to his tricks again, he'd barge in and save the damsel in distress.

The mere idea nearly made Damien laugh out loud, but he bit his lip instead. That's exactly what he'd do—he would help her but protect her, too. Then, at the right moment, he'd confess his feelings for her and hope to heck she didn't hate him. What could go wrong with a great plan like that?

A foam cup full of chocolate milk sat on Charley's desk. She kept her attention glued to Max's office, praying he wouldn't take his can of soda into the meeting.

When 8:30 neared, he pushed away from his desk and picked up his notepad and pen. He stood and stopped, glancing back at his desk.

She held her breath. *Don't take it!*

He turned and walked out of his office without his drink.

She released a sigh.

"Amanda," he called out. "I'll be back in about fifteen minutes."

Charley's redheaded friend nodded, her eyes glued to the small television on her desk as she watched a national news flash. Amanda's fingers gripped the pencil tight as she took notes.

Charley waited until 8:35 before she made her move. Acting as if it were an everyday occurrence for her to walk with a cup of chocolate milk in her hand, she smiled and tried not to spill the liquid. Once she reached Max's office, she went inside and closed the door. She quickly slipped off the second foam cup she'd put underneath the first, then poured Max's soda inside. Then she carefully poured the chocolate milk into the can. Placing the now-empty foam cup underneath the full one, she opened the door and casually walked back to her desk as if nothing had happened.

She scanned the room for anyone throwing curious stares her way. Surprisingly, nobody questioned her or even lifted a brow. She'd actually pulled it off! Of course, now she'd have to sit and wait until he drank it, and that would be the hardest part.

The clock on her desk ticked in slow motion. She even checked to see if the batteries were working. Ten minutes passed with her limbs trembling uncontrollably.

She wrung her hands and watched the conference room down the hall. When the door opened, her breathing accelerated. Max stepped out and she thought her racing heart would kill her.

Taking a deep breath, she tried to remain calm. Max walked into his room and sat behind his computer. He flipped open his notebook and glanced at the pages. His hand moved toward the can of soda.

She inhaled and held her breath.

As he continued to read, his fingers drummed on the side of the can.

Drink it!

Finally, he picked up the can and brought it to his mouth. Her own lips puckered as if trying to help him. He sipped. Almost immediately, he choked and spit out the liquid, spewing it across his desk. He wiped the back of his hand across his mouth. He lifted the drink to his nose and sniffed, then cursed loudly.

He jumped away from his desk and grabbed the drink, then hurried down the hall toward the break room, his eyes wide and his face pale.

Why did he look so panicked? Had he choked? Did he need help this very minute?

Now that Max had ingested the chemical, Charley needed to put herself in his way. She wanted to be the first person he saw when the chemical started working.

She pushed away from her desk and tried not to run down the hall. She slowed her steps, stopping at Amanda's desk, but her friend was busy on the phone. When Amanda looked up, Charley smiled and continued on.

Her legs shook as she walked to the break room. Her hand

trembled when she reached out and opened the door. Then she froze. Max leaned over the sink splashing water on his face—a face that looked too puffy to be his.

He turned and gazed her way, his lips now swollen and losing color. She gasped, ran to him, and grabbed his arm.

He coughed. "Call 9-1-1."

"Max? What's wrong?"

"I'm . . . allergic to . . . chocolate."

The blood left Charley's head and the room tilted around her. *What have I done?*

♡ Chapter Four

She could have killed Max.

Charley paced the floor in her front room. It was all Damien's fault! If he hadn't suggested switching the drinks, none of this would have happened. Yet, she was the one who asked for his help, wasn't she?

She huffed and turned around. The box of chocolates from the other day still sat on her end table, untouched. Her heart lodged in her throat and tears threatened. Why didn't anything go her way?

The knock at the door made her jump, and she spun around, glowering at the barrier as if it were something evil. When another knock sounded, she marched over and flung the door open.

There stood a grinning Adonis. She glared at him. "It didn't work, Damien."

The light in his brown eyes diminished and his smile disappeared. "What do you mean it didn't work?"

"Just what I said." With a sharp turn, she moved away and continued pacing across the living room floor.

Damien came in and closed the door, then strode to the couch and sat down. The red cotton polo-style shirt stretched across his wide chest, and his dark-wash jeans fit him too perfectly.

Charley folded her arms. "Why didn't you tell me Max is allergic to chocolate?"

Stretching his arm along the back of the sofa, he tilted his head and looked at her. "What are you talking about?"

"Max is allergic." She pointed to the box of chocolates. "That's the reason he didn't eat any yesterday."

"Really?"

"Don't tell me you didn't know."

"Honestly, Charley, I didn't know." Damien shrugged. "I thought everyone liked chocolate."

She stopped in front of him, moving her hands to her hips. "He's allergic."

His brows knit together. "And I tell you again, I didn't know."

"But you were his friend."

"I don't remember him being allergic to anything while we were friends in college."

Charley cringed at her quick temper. It really wasn't Damien's fault. He'd only been helping.

She exhaled deeply and plopped down beside him on the couch. His hand moved to her neck and massaged her tight muscles. She stiffened, ready to push him away, but his fingers soon soothed her anger. Gradually, her muscles relaxed, and she tilted her head forward to let his magic fingers do their work.

Although the quick massage relieved some of the stress in her body, the havoc in her mind wouldn't rest. Why couldn't she get anything right? She'd messed up from the very beginning. And why was Damien suddenly a sweet guy when just last week he was a womanizer?

"Damien, I could have killed him. Literally. I think I almost did." Her voice broke, and she fought the remorse threatening to consume her, making it hard to breathe.

She sniffed. "How am I supposed to win his heart if I make him ill?" A tear slipped down her cheek and she wiped it away.

"Hey," he said. "Come here."

She glanced at him just before he wrapped her in a tight hug. Once again, she stiffened, ready to resist, but when her cheek pressed against his chest, the steady rhythm of his heart relaxed her. Her traitorous body had a mind of its own and slumped against him. Then again, being cuddled by this big, strong Italian wasn't that bad, was it?

"Don't worry, mi amore, we won't mess up the next one."

"What should I do now?"

"Does he know you were the one who switched the drinks?"

"No."

"Keep it that way."

She lifted her head and peered into his eyes. Up this close, she could detect a mint scent in his breath. "Don't worry. I'm not stupid enough to announce my mistake."

His fingers stroked her cheek. Why was he looking at her like that? It was certainly different from the "come hither" stare he usually gave her. He almost seemed to genuinely like her, and she found herself staring into his warm brown eyes.

No! she thought, then pulled away. Damien was *not* the man for her. She wanted a man who could commit to marriage and family and God.

"How is he doing now?" Damien asked, reaching over to the end table for the box of chocolates. He opened it and took a piece, then popped it in his mouth.

"The paramedics gave him a shot of epinephrine before rushing him to the hospital. Everything must have been fine, because he came back to the office a few hours later. The bosses sent him home."

"I'm sorry."

The genuine concern in Damien's eyes thawed Charley's heart and lessened her anger. Her throat choked with a sob. Crying like a baby seemed like a good idea, but she blinked, fighting the tears. She shook her head. "I'm the one who's sorry. I didn't mean to accuse you."

He grabbed another chocolate. "Here, eat this. It'll make you feel better."

She tried not to smile, but the corner of her mouth tugged upward. How did he know chocolate made her happy?

He brought the piece of candy close to her mouth as if wanting to feed it to her. Her face warmed considerably. She quickly snatched the piece of candy from him.

Damien leaned back into the couch. "But now we need to do something else to get him to notice you."

"Can't you just fix us up on a blind date? After all, you are friends."

He shook his head. "No, we *were* friends."

"Why aren't you friends any longer?"

"Let's just say we didn't keep in touch after college."

"But couldn't you just—"

"Charley, it'd look better if you attracted him on your own. Besides, guys don't like to interfere with their friends' relationships. That's a woman's job."

She scowled. But he was right. "Okay, then, whatever I do to get his attention can't be something that might hurt him."

He chuckled. "No, we won't do that. We'll do something on that list of yours. What's the next way to win a man?"

She shrugged. "I'm a little stumped on this one."

"Why?"

"I'm supposed to get him a hard-to-find gift."

"Hmm." Damien scratched his chin, his gaze moving around the room. Then it stopped and his eyes widened. "I have it."

"You do? So soon?"

"Yes. This is perfect." He leaned toward her and clasped her hands. "You'll get him a plant."

"A plant? Why a plant?" She didn't think men liked plants that much. Then she remembered the plants decorating Damien's front room. But men who had plants nurtured them, cared for them, and loved them so they wouldn't die. Damien didn't seem the type of man who'd do something like that. He probably took such good care of them because they were part of a work experiment.

"What do you usually buy people who are in the hospital?" he asked. "Don't you get them flowers?"

"Yes."

"Well, I'm certain Mr. Sportsman wouldn't go for flowers, so I'm suggesting a plant."

Charley hesitated. "And guys like plants, right?"

"Does he live alone?"

"Yes, as far as I know."

"Then he'll probably need something to decorate his apartment. Look at my townhouse. The plants brighten up the place. I've studied a lot about plants due to the inventions of GIO Products, and I've learned that they do more than just decorate. Some actually send off a scent that will make a person feel better."

"Promise?"

"Yes."

"But I have to get him a hard-to-find gift. Plants aren't that hard to find."

He nodded. His finger tapped against the cute little dimple in his chin. "Then don't get him just an ordinary plant. Get him a tropical plant."

She lifted her brows. "A tropical plant? That sounds good."

"I know exactly where you can find one. There's this little shop in the center of Main Street that'll be perfect. If they don't have what you're looking for, they'll order one for you." He stood and held out his hand. "Shall we go?"

She grinned, wondering if she should go with him. It was strange how quickly he'd sneaked into her life. Right now he acted like her best friend. But finding a plant for Max was something she wanted to do on her own.

She shook her head. "I can do this myself."

"If that's how you want it." His hand dropped to his side, his smile fading.

Her heart twisted. She'd hurt his feelings, and although they were new friends, she didn't want it to be over so soon. She jumped to her feet and reached for his hand. "Don't be upset with me."

"It's all right, mi amore. I just have to find a way to pass the rest of my afternoon."

"Promise you won't be mad?"

"I promise." He smiled and squeezed her hand. "Now go get that plant, and make it a good one."

She smiled at him. "I will."

Hard-to-Find Gifts

"I'll call it the 'love fern,'" Charley said with a giggle. She ordered the plant online, then clicked off the computer. Going to the plant shop Damien told her about certainly helped, but the plants just weren't what she wanted. It had to be eye-catching—a plant that would look good on Max's desk. In a couple of days they'd deliver the pretty green and silver fern. This time she signed her name on the card so he'd know whom it was from.

She needed to get rid of her shyness. It wouldn't be that hard. She'd tell him the plant was to wish him a quick recovery. After all, she was the one who had called 9-1-1 and stayed with him until the ambulance came. Of course, she'd thought he was dying at the time, and that she was his accidental killer.

Hopefully the next few days would pass quickly. In the meantime, she'd try to talk to Max as much as she could; well, maybe she'd just smile at him instead. Just thinking about talking to him made her stomach twist in knots.

But the next few days didn't fly as she had hoped. Max and the sports producers were out of the office a great deal, filming a segment with the local basketball team. It was utterly impossible to work without seeing his charming grin and hearing his baritone laughter. She'd also missed his knee-weakening cologne, and she found herself walking by his office every so often just to sniff inside.

The day she waited for came, and Max sat in his office as though the universe knew her plan and wanted to help. The brown-uniformed delivery driver brought in a large plant wrapped in yellow cellophane. Charley's hands shook when the driver handed the plant to Max. She moved from the file cabinet to her chair so she wouldn't end up on the floor like warm JELL-O.

People gathered around as Max opened his gift. She couldn't see the plant so she rose from her seat, trying to peek over their heads. Laughter filled Max's office, and her heart sank. *What's so funny?*

Charley breathed a sigh of relief when everyone finally left and she could see where he'd put the plant. When she noticed the color, she inhaled sharply. It wasn't the green-and-silver-leafed plant she'd ordered; the leaves were dark green and shiny, and a couple of white, yellow, and pink flowers protruded from the center of the plant. This was *not* the love fern she'd ordered!

Then she saw the card in Max's hand. She couldn't let him read it. Not now.

She pushed away from her desk, stood, and promptly tripped over her small garbage can, spilling its contents, but she didn't care. She hurried around desks, making her way toward Max's office, and just as she turned the corner, the senior editor cut her off by stepping into his office first. Charley skidded to a halt and groaned.

Doug Edwards laughed as he saw the gift, his large gut shaking like Santa's bowl full of jelly. "What have you got there, Max?"

"Charley sent me this plant." He glanced at the card. "It says, 'For a speedy recovery.'"

Edwards shrugged. "Well, I have to admit, it definitely adds color to your office." His sarcastic tone made her want to kick him in the shins.

She held her breath, waiting for Max's comment. When he gave the older man a scowl, she breathed a sigh of relief.

"Doug, it's a great plant. The tag says it's called a Christmas rose. I've never seen anything like it, and I'm sure Charley went through a lot of trouble to get it for me."

Edwards grinned. "Yeah, I bet she searched really hard to find it. She's not the research producer for nothing."

Charley couldn't stop the smile from stretching across her face. Max liked it. Her heart beat to life again.

Now would be the perfect time to talk to him, but just as she said a silent prayer for courage, Amanda waved to her, motioning her over.

Charley shook her head. Amanda pointed to the clock on the wall. Then Charley remembered. They had a deadline. The five o'clock news was approaching fast, with still so much to do. There would be no time to talk with Max now.

She crept back to her desk and sat at her computer. Amanda came over and handed her a stack of papers. Charley smiled, knowing she could finally focus on work, with the plant delivery out of the way.

Deep in concentration as she and Amanda went over some items for the evening broadcast, she didn't see Max approaching until he was just a few feet from her desk.

"Hey, Charley."

"Huh?" She glanced his way, her heart hammering against her ribs. "Oh, hello, Max. How are you feeling?"

"Just fine, thanks. And thanks for the plant." He gave her a wide smile and then strode back to his office.

Amanda nudged Charley with her elbow. "Way to go, girl."

Charley's face went red. "Well, I felt awful about the reaction he had the other day from that chocolate."

"Yeah, just terrible, wasn't it? And who knew his allergy was that bad? I wonder how chocolate milk got in his cup when he'd been drinking root beer."

Charley shrugged but kept her mouth closed. She wondered if Amanda suspected she had been the one to almost kill Max.

The rest of the day passed quickly, and Charley kept busy until quitting time. When Max walked out of his office and turned off the light, he looked her way and smiled. He held up the plant. "I'm going to take this home and put it by my front window where there's plenty of sunlight."

Her heart leapt. "That's a great place to keep it."

Max had made her day, her evening, and even her year.

She practically skipped out to her car, and when she walked

from her vehicle toward her townhouse, the bounce in her step hadn't disappeared. Her face hurt from the constant smile, but she didn't care. Things were working perfectly. She'd have to thank Damien.

Instead of going home, she went straight to Damien's door and knocked. Inside, his musical whistle rang through the house.

When he opened the door and looked at her, his smile widened. Happiness overwhelmed her and she couldn't keep from flinging her arms around his neck and hugging him tight. She kissed his cheek and he caught his breath in a quick inhale. His arms wound around her waist, bringing her closer to him. His musky scent stirred flutters in her stomach, and even the beat of her heart quickened.

She withdrew from his embrace and looked at him. "Your suggestion worked."

He pulled her into his apartment and kicked the door closed with his foot. "What happened?"

His voice sounded deeper than usual and his brown eyes twinkled, stirring warmth in her chest. She scolded herself for reacting this way. "They delivered my plant to Max's office today and he liked it."

Had his smile just wavered? No, it couldn't have. He was excited for her.

"Really? I thought you bought it the other day."

"No, I ordered it. The delivery driver brought it today." She pouted for a brief moment. "It wasn't exactly the plant I'd ordered, but he liked it anyhow."

Damien's black eyebrows rose. "Really? What did you order?"

"The plant I ordered was called hunter's robe."

"What did they send?"

She shrugged. "It was a weird-looking plant with shiny

green leaves, and a strange white, yellow, and pink flower." She chuckled. "It was definitely tropical."

"Do you know what it's called?"

"Christmas rose, I think."

His eyes widened. "Christmas rose, you say?"

"Yes, why? Have you heard of it?"

He nodded. "If it's the plant I'm thinking about—" He paused and covered his mouth.

She smacked his shoulder playfully. "Damien, tell me. What do you know about this plant?"

"Charley, honey, I think you gave him a . . . a . . . a poisonous plant."

Her heart hit the floor. "What? Why would a plant with a name like 'Christmas rose' be poisonous?"

He turned to walk into his den. She followed, sick with dread. There was no way she could have done something that awful to Max—again!

On the far side of the wall sat Damien's computer desk. He bent over the machine, his fingers flying across the keyboard. She leaned closer, studying the websites as they popped on the screen. Within minutes, he'd found a site for poisonous plants. Another click displayed the picture of the Christmas rose.

"Is this it?" he asked over his shoulder.

Her heart sank. "Oh, no," she muttered. "I've done it again."

Chapter Five ♡

The color faded from Charley's face and she brought her hands up to cover her cheeks. Tears swam in her eyes, wrenching Damien's heart. Her body swayed, and he reached out to clutch her shoulders, steadying her.

"Charley, it's going to be all right. We'll just call Max and tell him—"

"No." A sob tore from her throat. "We can't call Max. He can't know I made a mistake . . . again."

"You didn't. The mistake was made by the shop."

"You don't understand. I can't mess up with Max. He's supposed to be different." She pulled away from him and sank into the swivel chair by the computer, her eyes looking blankly toward the screen.

He knelt beside her and ran his fingers over her knee. "Although the plant is poisonous, I'm sure he won't eat the leaves or the flowers. That's the only way it can hurt him."

She leaned forward, her gaze moving across the screen as she read the Internet article. "It also says it may cause a rash."

Damien sighed and ran his fingers through his hair. "True, but I don't think he'll be playing with the leaves, either."

"But what if—"

"Charley, please stop worrying."

She swung her head around to face him, her eyes wide. "We have to do something."

"What do you suggest?"

His chest constricted from the sadness touching her eyes. He wanted to take her into his arms and comfort her, and yet he couldn't. He wouldn't be able to stand a rejection from her. Besides, he wanted to prove to her, and himself, that he could just be her friend. He liked her for her mind and her sense of humor, especially the way she made him laugh.

Her shoulders lifted in a shrug. "We could go get it from his house."

She was so cute, even when she wasn't trying to be funny.

"And what would you say to him when he greets you at his door?" he asked.

"Well, I was thinking we could wait until he leaves, then get it."

Damien blinked and shook his head. "I don't think I heard you right. Are you talking about breaking and entering?"

The corner of her mouth raised in a grin. "Maybe."

He chuckled. "You are serious."

She lifted herself from the chair and paced the length of his living room. Her teeth pulled on her bottom lip, as she did the nervous nibble he enjoyed watching.

"Actually, I am serious." She stopped and met his gaze. "I need to get into his house while he's away and take the plant."

Damien stood and folded his arms. "You've forgotten one thing, mi amore. How are you going to do this?" He took two steps toward her. "Do you even know where he lives?"

The color in her cheeks darkened. "Yes."

He wasn't going to ask how she knew. Not yet, anyway. He didn't want to think of her as Max's stalker. Then again, that thought only made him want to laugh.

He nodded. "Second, do you know his schedule? How will you know when he leaves his house?"

"I thought about watching him—a stakeout, so to speak."

"Hmm. And who'll be your partner in crime while you're ransacking his house? Who'll watch out for you?"

Her eyes softened and she smiled. "You."

How did he know she was going to say that? Yet, the hammering in his heart gave him the answer. Illegal or not, he'd help her. She owed him big-time now, and he'd find a way to collect.

"Fine."

She squealed and threw her arms around him. He buried his face in her neck, inhaling her berry scent, the scent that drove him crazy.

He didn't want to let her go, but she pulled away.

"Let me go home and change first. I think we should both wear dark clothes, don't you?"

"You're really getting into this, aren't you?" He smiled. "I suppose we'll fit right into character when the police come to arrest us."

She slapped his shoulder. "Would you stop thinking so negatively? This is going to work. I just know it."

A few hours later, they drove up to Max's house. Only one small light lit his porch. Charley leaned toward Damien as she looked out his window. "This is perfect. His house is dark and his car isn't in the driveway."

Her voice pulled Damien from his thoughts and he looked at her. "Are you sure?"

"Yes." She sat back in her seat. "Now drive over there." She motioned her hand to a spot on the street shadowed by a large oak tree.

He drove the car alongside the curb and turned off the engine. At midnight, not a lot of neighbors were out and about. Damien thanked his lucky stars for the privacy of the night, especially the half-moon.

Once he unfastened his seatbelt, he turned and took hold of Charley's hands. Her soft skin beckoned him to caress her fingers and arm. Good grief, working this close with her would cause havoc in his head!

"Are you certain about this?" he asked her.

"Positive."

He sighed. "Then let's go, Bonnie."

Her eyebrow rose. "I'm right beside you, Clyde."

Damien held her hand as she led the way. When she crouched low, he crouched. When she stopped, so did he. The theme to *Mission Impossible* played in his head, and he could barely refrain from laughing. Finally, he and Charley stood with their backs against the side of Max's house near the front-room window.

She tilted her head, looking up at the window. She pursed her lips. "Great. It's too high. How are we supposed to peek in now?"

Damien knelt on one knee in front of her and motioned his head over his shoulder. "Climb on."

Her eyes widened. "Climb on your shoulders?"

"Yes."

She walked around him. "I—I don't know how."

"Just step on my knee and swing your other leg over my shoulders. Haven't you been on a horse before?"

"Once as a child, but—"

"There's no difference. Hurry, you're wasting time."

When she placed her black tennis shoe on his knee, he helped her with the other leg, swinging it around his neck. The moment she was in place, he slowly lifted her to the window. He clamped his hands around her legs to keep her from falling.

"Can you see it?" he asked with a tight voice.

"Not yet."

He gritted his teeth. Why was he going out of his way to do things for her when he'd never have her heart? Good ol' Maxwell would have it. What Damien helped Charley do tonight was something the sports anchorman would never do. Damien enjoyed being with her, and he wished she could see that the man in front of her appreciated her more than the one she'd set her sights on.

"I think I see it," she whispered.

"Where is it?"

"By his television."

"Is it by a window?"

"Yes, but really, Damien, I don't see how we're going to get it without breaking in. Too bad it isn't the middle of summer. At least a window might be open."

Despite it being early December, Damien realized he wasn't cold at all. Charley's closeness kept the winter chill away.

"So now what do we do?" he asked.

"Let me down."

He knelt on the concrete and lifted her legs off his shoulders then set her on the ground. "So, what do you have planned now?"

"I don't know, but I know I have to do something. I can't let him keep that plant in his house if it's poisonous. If he touches it, he'll get a rash, and let's hope he doesn't try and taste it." She shivered.

"Only an idiot would eat it, Charley."

She elbowed him in the ribs. "You know what I mean."

He sighed and raked his fingers through his hair. "I think you'll just have to walk up to his door and explain to him that the shop mixed up the plants."

"No. I can't."

"Why not?"

"Well, because I'd have to talk to him."

"So, talk to him."

Charley shook her head. "It's too soon." She grasped Damien's hand. "You go talk to him."

"Honey, I'm not the one who sent him the wrong plant."

She scowled. "It was by mistake."

"Exactly, so I don't see a problem."

Her sorrowful expression tugged at his heartstrings again, and he heard himself say, "Maybe I can pick the lock on his front door."

Her eyes widened. "Can you do that without getting caught?"

"Aw, you do care about me." He smiled and stroked her cold cheek.

She rolled her eyes. "Damien, please concentrate. What are we going to do?"

From up the street, the sound of a car engine roared through the silence of the night. Damien grabbed Charley around the waist and pinned her against the side of the house, hoping the passing car wouldn't notice the prowlers. Instead of driving by, the vehicle pulled into the driveway and the engine killed.

Just their luck. Max was home.

After the car lights turned off, Damien ducked and tugged on Charley's hand, leading her around the corner to the large bush bordering Max's property.

She gave a sharp inhale. "Damien, that's Max."

"I know."

"Do you think he saw us?"

He crouched low, pulling her with him. "Shh, be quiet."

She snuggled against him, her arms tightening around his upper arm. "Can you see anything?"

He peeked over the bush. "Only shadows." He kept his eyes on the sidewalk. Soon two figures appeared. "Somebody's with him."

"Who is it?"

He waited until the woman's high-heeled shoes touched the concrete. Narrowing his eyes, he studied the slender feminine figure. When Max and the woman stopped underneath the porch light, Damien breathed a sigh of relief. It wasn't the woman he'd expected. Of course, he hadn't seen *that* particular woman in a long time, but the betrayal was still as raw as if he'd seen them wrapped in each other's arms yesterday.

Beside him, Charley tugged on his arm. "Answer me. Who is it?"

"A woman," he said softly.

Her body stiffened and his heart clenched. It hurt to see how much this bothered Charley.

"Is it his mother?" she whispered.

Damien switched his attention back to the couple at the door. The curvy young woman certainly didn't look like anyone's mother.

"Well?" Charley asked, her voice rising.

"Unless he was conceived when his mother was five, I seriously doubt it."

"So, she's an older woman?" she asked.

"I can't exactly tell, but she might be."

Damien waited until the door closed and a light glowed inside the house. Then he stood and brought Charley with him.

He hooked his arm around her shoulders and pulled her against his side as they crept back to the window.

Her arms remained around his waist as if she didn't want to let go. The softness of her cuddled against him was almost his undoing. He tightened his jaw.

"Damien, can you see what's going on?"

Since he was taller, he didn't have to climb on anything to see inside. Right away he spotted Max and the woman, and when he realized what they were doing, he couldn't keep from smiling. Max's date stood by the flowered plant, stroking the leaves as she pressed her nose in close to the bud for a sniff.

"Can you see what they're doing?" Charley repeated.

"Yes, and it's not good."

"Is she in his arms? Are they kissing?"

"Well, not exactly."

She tugged on his black hoodie. "What exactly are they doing?"

"He's showing her the plant."

She slapped his arm. "Don't lie."

"I'm not. They're standing right next to the plant."

"The woman is looking at it?" Her voice held a hint of sarcasm.

"Yes. She's touching it, smelling it, and pretty soon, she'll get sick."

Charley chuckled softly at first, but when the chuckles turned into loud guffaws, she turned and buried her face in Damien's chest. Closing his eyes, he tightened his arms around her and breathed deeply, cherishing the moment because he knew it wouldn't last long. "I think you should go in and break it up."

She lifted her head. "Why would I want to break it up? I want that woman to keep touching the plant. Then she'll get sick, and I'll replace her."

A lock of hair had fallen across her face, so Damien pushed it back behind her ear. He smiled at her. "You're not being very nice."

She shrugged. "All's fair in love and war, right?"

He arched an eyebrow. Was the real Charley showing through? He rather liked this passionate side of her. "Yes, I suppose you're right."

"So come on, let's go home. I'll tell him about the plant tomorrow."

"What if Max starts touching and smelling the plant?"

"That's a chance I'll have to take, right?"

Damien gazed into her eyes. The moonlight touched them, making them sparkle just the way he liked. What had this woman done to him?

He shook his head. "Come on, let's go before we get caught."

Hunched over her desk, Charley focused on her computer screen, deep in thought as she researched the next news story. From down the hall, voices rang out, calling Max's name. She jerked to a sitting position and glanced at her clock. Only half an hour late. She looked his way as he came into view. Red blotches covered his face, and he looked like he wore purple lip balm.

Inwardly, she groaned. Time to tell him about the plant mix-up.

She wrung her hands against her stomach. Would he blame her? He still didn't know she had switched his root beer for chocolate milk, and she wasn't about to tell him, either.

Charley tried to force herself off the chair and away from her desk, but her feet remained rooted to the floor. Luckily, her fingers still worked, so she turned to her computer and clicked open her email. Pulling up Max's email address, she nibbled on her bottom lip as her heartbeat hammered against her ribs. *Please don't blame me . . .*

> Max, the shop I purchased your plant from just contacted me that there was a mix-up. Instead of the fern I'd ordered, they sent you a poisonous plant. Please use caution and don't touch the yellow and pink flower. Also, don't keep the plant indoors as it might cause nausea. Please forgive me for this mistake. I've already contacted the owners of this company to complain. Let me know if there is anything else I can do for you. Your friend, Charley

She read over the email again before sending it. Closing her eyes, she massaged her forehead and prayed Max would understand and forgive her. What if he didn't? She snapped her eyes open and stared at the computer screen. No, that wasn't an option. He *had* to forgive her.

With a deep sigh, she decided to let things happen as they would. If Max forgave her, that would be her sign to proceed with the remaining eight ways to win her man.

Her phone rang and she jumped. She placed a hand over her crazily beating heart. "Hello?"

"Hello, mi amore."

"Is this Damien?"

"Sure is, honey, unless you know another Italian man who uses that endearment when he talks to you."

His deep voice stirred emotions in Charley she didn't want to deal with right now. "Hi," she replied with a sigh.

"Well, how did it go? Did you talk to Max?"

What's wrong with Damien's voice? Had he caught a cold while helping her spy last night in the winter temperatures?

"Yes and no. I let him know about the plant, but I haven't talked to him."

"What did you do this time?" He sounded like a father scolding a child.

"I emailed him."

"What did you tell him?"

"Just the truth—that the store mixed up the plants and sent him the poisonous one. I told him what effects he might get, but by looking at him today, I can see he's already figured that out."

Laughter pealed from the other end. "You don't sound very upset."

"Of course I'm mad, but, well, he deserves this, I think."

"How do you figure that?"

"Because he took out the wrong girl last night."

Damien laughed even harder.

"He'll learn," she told him.

"You're awful, Charlene Randall, just awful. But that's what I love about you."

Love? Nah, he didn't mean it *that* way. "Well, I don't usually act this way, but I can't help it. Not today."

"You don't need to make any excuses, Charley. You can be yourself with me, you know."

"Yes, I know." Her heart did a silly little leap. "Hey, I've got to hang up now. Talk to you later."

"Have a nice day, mi amore."

"You too."

When she hung up, Charley was still smiling. Lately, Damien had been making her smile a lot, and she was glad they were friends. He was no longer the teasing neighbor next door, but the man she could confide in. The man that didn't mind taking the chance of going to jail with her.

She extended her neck, releasing the kinks, then turned back to her computer to get some work done. On the screen, she could see someone behind her. Still, Amanda's voice made her jump.

"I have it all planned out."

Charley swiveled in her chair and faced her supervisor. "What do you have planned?"

"How I'm going to hook you and Max up at the office party."

Charley's stomach fluttered nervously. "Oh, really?"

Amanda's smile spread from ear to ear. "Do you want to hear about it?"

Several months before, Amanda had helped with another soon-to-be boyfriend, and although the results were disastrous, it was fun while it lasted. "Sure. This ought to be good for a laugh or two."

Amanda rolled her eyes. "You'll thank me when it's over, I promise."

The more Charley listened, the faster her heart beat. Amanda was serious. Charley was going to actually *speak* to Max, and there would be no excuses this time.

Chapter Six ♡

Charley stared at her pasty face in the mirror and frowned. Her nervous stomach wasn't cut out for catching a man—a hunk of a man, for that matter. This time she could *not* mess things up. That's what worried her. With her track record, she knew it was almost impossible.

She pinched her cheeks, but the raspberry color that appeared in stark contrast made her look like she had a fever. Maybe she did. She placed a hand on her forehead. No. Her skin felt normal. If she wasn't sick, why did her body tremble?

Taking careful, steady steps so as not to disturb her stomach, she made her way back into her bedroom and lowered herself face down on the bed. No way could she go to the company Christmas party tonight. Amanda planned to sabotage Max's date so he could spend time with Charley at the party instead. A confident Amanda actually had Charley believing it'd happen. This might just be her night.

But now, well, she couldn't go. What if she passed out? She'd look like a fool. It'd be high school all over again. Maybe the queasiness had nothing to do with her tense nerves. What if something was seriously wrong with her?

Yeah, I have the chicken-out disease, she thought. *I'm just a pathetic loser!*

Soon, the tightness in her head convinced her a cold was coming on. She couldn't go to the party and get everyone sick.

She frowned and rolled to her back. Okay, so maybe she wasn't as sick as she tried to believe, but the thought of talking to Max nearly frightened her to death. That man was way out of her league. She'd faint if he turned his beautiful eyes on her. She couldn't lose consciousness at a company party. As shy as she was, there'd be no way she'd be able to show up for work after that.

But could she give up so soon? Her whole purpose for trying the article's ten steps was to see if she could get Max and keep him longer than three months. Hadn't she wanted to date him since high school? Wasn't it about time Charlene Randall went after and got what she wanted?

She stared at the ceiling, willing the churning in her stomach to stop. She took deep breaths through her mouth to ease the rolling tension. As her eyelids grew heavy, she closed them, but then a knock sounded at the door.

"Charley? Are you there?"

Damien.

She rolled her weak body off the bed and carefully walked to the front door, her hands splayed over her stomach. With a shaky hand, she released the latch and unlocked the door. "Hi."

His eyes widened as his gaze slid from the top of her head to her bare feet. "What's wrong with you? Don't you have a party tonight?"

She groaned and stepped away from the door, weaving her way to the couch in the front room. She plopped down and sighed.

"No, I *had* a party tonight."

He walked inside and shut the door. "Have you caught something?"

"Yes."

He stopped. "Is it contagious?"

"Sure, if you're a chicken."

His dark eyebrows rose. "I don't understand."

He came closer until his knees bumped the edge of the couch. Charley peeked at him from beneath half-closed lids. Once again, he looked as if he'd walked straight out of the Nordstrom catalog. Today he wore sharp-creased gray trousers and a cream-colored shirt that hung loosely over his muscled torso. With the two buttons he'd left undone, she caught a glimpse of his muscular neck. He could have been a nobleman off the front cover of an eighteenth-century romance novel. *If only . . .*

She covered her eyes, trying to ignore his handsomeness, but memories from the other night floated through her mind. He'd been so sweet, so caring, so willing to help. Just thinking about how he went out of his way made her heart warm.

His hand touched her forehead, and she jumped.

"You don't feel like you have a fever."

"I think I'm catching a head cold."

He left her side and hurried out of her house, leaving the front door open. Slowly, she lowered her hands and watched the door. Minutes later he returned with a glass of water and two pills.

"Take this."

"What is it?"

"It's a decongestant. It'll clear your head really fast."

"Well, if you're sure . . ." She gave him a half smile, then swallowed the pills and downed the water.

He took the empty glass from her. "Great. Now let's get you ready for your party."

Charley groaned and shook her head, covering her eyes with her hands again. "You don't understand, Damien. The reason I'm sick is because I'm scared of going tonight and making a fool out of myself."

His chuckle made her sneak a peek at him from between her fingers. His brown eyes sparkled. "Mi amore, you have nothing to worry about. Once Max gets to know the real you, he'll fall head over heels."

She lowered her hands and scowled. "I doubt it, and even if he does, I don't want him *falling* in any way. That could be dangerous."

The corners of his lips turned up as he bent over and grasped her arm. "Nonsense. All you need is a little encouragement."

"No, all I need is a fairy godmother."

He laughed. "Will a fairy godfather do?"

"I guess, since you're the only option I have."

He grabbed her hands and pulled her up. Luckily, her stomach didn't protest this time.

"I assume you've already taken a shower." He leaned into her and sniffed her neck.

Warm tingles spread through her body and she had to hold herself back from leaning into him more. Goose bumps ran over her arms and she giggled.

"Yes, you have," he said. "You smell like berries, but I could get you a perfume from my work that compliments your scent."

"You think GIO products are better than what I use?"

"You'll never know unless you try them."

He pulled her into the bathroom and positioned her in front of the mirror. Her pale skin shone like a beacon, making her blue eyes appear much larger. *Ugh!* Charley thought. *I'll never look pretty enough for Max.*

"First thing we need to do is let down your hair."

He gently removed the hairband from her hair, releasing her ponytail. Then he picked up her brush and ran it through her hair. The gentleness of his actions made her close her eyes and relax. Soon his fingers threaded through her locks, massaging, stroking warmth back into her scalp. *Oh, he's good.*

When he took her by the shoulders and turned her around, she looked at him. Up this close, his eyes appeared darker than she'd first imagined, almost black.

He pushed her to the toilet seat and made her sit. Thankfully, the lid was down or she would have fallen in.

"Now be still and let me do my job."

Once his fingers made contact with her hair, she closed her eyes again. He used gel and hairspray, ratting and pulling, and she enjoyed the tender way he touched her. When she realized her thoughts were not on Max, she scolded herself. *Think about Max.*

She tried to imagine that Damien's hands were Max's. What would Max wear tonight? Would he talk to her, dance with her, take her outside to walk in the moonlight? Should she make the first move? No. He'd definitely have to do it.

Charley could almost feel the texture of his blond hair as she twirled her finger around a strand. She could almost smell his cologne. She imagined running her fingers through his hair and caressing his close-shaven jaw. Soon, Max's face was replaced with Damien's. His eyes would be closed as she touched his hair and his face. A satisfied grin would pull at his mouth, a mouth she wanted to kiss.

"Now that's done, let's move on."

Damien's voice made her dream disappear and she almost let out a disappointed groan. As he stepped away, she forced herself back to reality and opened her heavy lids in time to see him snatch up her makeup case. He pulled it over closer on the counter.

She blinked and shook her head. "You're going to do my makeup?"

He folded his arms across his massive chest. "You don't think I can do an adequate job?"

"I didn't say that."

"You certainly implied it." He grinned. "Do you trust me?"

"I let you do my hair, didn't I?"

He laughed. "Close your eyes and let me help."

Once again, Charley let her eyelids drift close and concentrated on the sense of touch—his touch. Soft, gentle, warm.

He used the sponge to dab on her foundation. The brush breezed across her cheeks when he applied the blush, although she didn't think she'd need it tonight. It took a little longer for Damien to stroke the eye shadow across her lids and apply some eyeliner.

She tried to imagine Max again, but Damien's masculine scent enveloped her, making her want to bury her face in his neck and stay in his arms forever.

"Here. I'll let you do this."

She jerked back from his voice and snapped her eyes open. She cursed herself for letting her thoughts get carried away again. What was wrong with her, anyway? Why couldn't she focus on Max?

He held the tube of mascara in front of her. Charley stood and faced the mirror and froze. *Wow!* Good thing he wasn't charging her. It would cost a fortune to get all this done in a salon.

She leaned closer to the mirror and thickened her eyelashes with the mascara brush. When she was finished, she turned to face him. He took out a lip pencil and glanced at her lips.

"Pucker for me, baby."

She laughed.

"That's not a pucker."

"Then quit making me laugh."

Damien was adorable. He'd make some girl really happy when he decided to settle down. But that was the problem—he probably wouldn't ever settle down.

Charley puckered for him and stayed still while he outlined her lips. When he took the tube of lipstick and brought it to her mouth, she relaxed her lips and let him apply it. His eyes narrowed as he worked.

"Perfect." He finally stepped away, giving her a self-assured grin.

She rolled her eyes heavenward. "You're boasting."

He clasped his hand around hers and pulled her into her bedroom. "Now let's pick out a dress."

"Nothing too fancy. I don't want to stand out."

"Oh, but I think you should."

She grimaced. "Really, Damien, I don't think—"

He stopped suddenly and she bumped into him. A scowl took over his handsome features.

"Now listen, Charley. Do you want my help or not? I thought we were trying to get Mr. Jock to notice you."

"We are, but I don't want it to look obvious."

"So, do you want my help?" He held up his hands.

She shrugged. "Well, that was the idea."

"Then you're going to have to wear what I tell you."

She expelled a heavy breath, her heart racing once again. "All right."

He wandered into her walk-in closet and sorted through her dresses. She stepped just inside the room to watch. When his hand stopped on the glittery red gown, her heart sank and she groaned. She hadn't worn it since her mother purchased it for her two years ago for Christmas.

Damien brought it over to her. "I like this one."

"Then you wear it." She folded her arms across her chest.

"It's not my size. Now go put it on."

"Damien, I can't—"

"No, you *won't* wear it." He sighed. "There's a difference."

"But you don't understand. That dress is . . . uh . . . it's . . ."

"It's what?" He held it up. "Gorgeous? Perhaps you don't like it because it's the perfect color for you?"

"No, it's just not me." The bodice hugged her chest a little more than she thought proper, and the slit in the skirt went a bit above her knee. The fact was, she didn't have enough body—or courage, for that matter—for that dress. Charley's mother's nickname for her when she was younger was "Scrawny," and she figured the name still fit.

Damien's smile widened. "This dress is more you than you realize. Go put it on."

She huffed. "No."

"If I have to dress you myself, I will." He stood firm. "Charley, we don't have long to argue. The party starts in half an hour."

"But—"

"No 'but's. Just put the dress on."

When she didn't move, he grabbed the end of her shirt and pulled it up. Quickly, before he could see anything she didn't want shown, she clamped her elbows to her sides to keep the material from riding up any farther. Her heart pounded out of control and she glared at him.

"I mean it, Charley."

"Fine! Give me the stupid dress."

She yanked it out of his hand and marched into the bathroom. Grumbling under her breath, she hastily donned the evening gown. Long, straight sleeves hugged her arms, and just as she had remembered, the bodice fit snugly.

When Charley moved, the slit displayed more leg than she

was comfortable with. She had to admit, though, that the red dress brought color to her face, and the hairstyle Damien had created looked good on her. It didn't fit her personality, but now she looked quite sophisticated, and the bold dress matched the hairstyle perfectly.

"You're taking too long," Damien called from the other room.

"Be patient. I'll be right out."

After taking a deep breath, Charley opened the door and stepped out. Damien's gaze moved over her slowly.

He whistled and shook his head. "Woman, you are stunning."

Her cheeks burned. "Thanks." She held her hands away from her sides. "But this is your creation."

Damien grinned, then moved close and touched her chin, his thumb gently stroking the skin. "Just make sure you're back by midnight. You'll turn into a pumpkin if you aren't."

She laughed, then threw her arms around him and gave him a hug. "You're the greatest. Do you know that?"

"Yes, but I get rather bored telling it to myself all the time."

She placed a light kiss on his cheek and felt his body stiffen. For some reason, it seemed to bother him when she kissed his check. But she had more important things to worry about right now. "I owe you for this," she said.

He looked at her tenderly, but soon he cleared his throat and the expression disappeared.

"Are you ready?" he asked.

"Let me just put on my nylons and I'll be ready."

"Now remember, men love compliments."

Suddenly, she recalled the Internet article. It said, "Give a man compliments." Damien was right. She would do that. "That's good. So what do you think I should say?"

"Tell him how sharp he looks in his suit. Tell him how the color compliments his eyes. Tell him you like his smile, enjoy hearing his voice when he's on the news, and most importantly, tell him . . ." He paused and his grin widened.

"What?" she urged.

"Tell him what a nice butt he has."

She slapped Damien's arm. "You're awful."

"No, I'm serious. Guys like it when women tell us we look nice." He laughed. "Okay. I'm going now." He kissed her cheek. "Have a good time at the ball, and if you need a designated driver, you know my number."

She shooed him with her hands. "Sorry to disappoint you, but I don't drink."

"That's right. You're too churchy to drink, right?"

She pulled her shoulders straight. "Right, and don't you forget it."

He nodded. "It's good to meet a woman who is true to her faith."

Curious about his comment, she studied his eyes. "Damien, do you go to church?"

Chuckling, he folded his arms and leaned back against the wall. "One time in my life I did."

"What church did you attend?"

"I'm a Mormon—or what you would call a Jack Mormon."

"Really? What happened to make you stop going?"

He stared at her for the longest time. She didn't dare prod, only because she could tell he was seriously thinking about her question. Finally, he shrugged and his smile disappeared.

"Let's just say *life* happened."

She exhaled deeply and moved closer to him, resting her hand on his shoulder. "Whenever you want to talk about it, I'm here."

"Thanks." He pulled away from the wall, dropping his hands

to his sides. "Well, have a great time, Cinderella."

"I'll try my hardest." In her mind, she finished with, *". . . Prince Charming."* Then she reminded herself he certainly was *not* her Prince Charming.

After he left her townhouse, she finished getting ready. Her heart pounded in a different rhythm now, but she didn't know if it was the exchange she'd just had with Damien, or because she was going to force herself to talk to Max tonight.

She tried to breathe slower, convincing herself the excitement bubbling inside her was for Max. In less than fifteen minutes she would see Maxwell Harrington's reaction to the new Charlene Randall.

Give him compliments

The squishy heels made Charley's ankles wobble. The last time her legs shook this bad was last summer's earthquake, which had lasted for what seemed like hours.

Charley walked into the Richmond Hotel and headed toward the ballroom. As she checked her coat, she heard Christmas music, clinking glasses, and voices raised in laughter. Smells of cinnamon and pine assaulted her senses, and she sneezed repeatedly. But at least there was no tightness in her sinus any longer; the pills Damien had given her had worked wonders.

When Charley stepped into the ballroom, she saw dozens of people from her office, but there was no sign of Max.

"Charley? Is that you?"

She turned toward Amanda's voice. Her supervisor stood with a group of coworkers, all holding alcoholic beverages. Charley gave them her best smile and walked their way. "Hi, Amanda."

"Oh, my goodness," Amanda said. "Look at you."

Charley blushed. "Yes, I'm aware I'm out of character, but—"

"You look fabulous." Amanda grabbed hold of her hand and squeezed. "You're going to knock 'em dead tonight."

Charley let out an uneasy laugh. "Oh, let's hope nobody dies. That wouldn't be a good thing, especially with my luck." She scanned her friend's attire. Amanda always looked great in black, and the satin dress fit her personality.

"So, Charley, have you seen Max yet?"

"No. Have you?"

"No."

Charley frowned and clasped her hands against her stomach. "I hope nothing bad has happened to him."

Amanda laughed and waved her hand through the air. "Oh, you know Max. He's got to make a grand entrance." She reached out and touched Charley's sleeve. "But I think you've taken that special moment away from him. You look good, woman."

"Thanks. This is my neighbor's creation."

Her friend's eyes widened. "Seriously? Is he for real?"

"Yes, he is. He just works at GIO Products, so he knows all about a woman's needs."

Amanda shook her head and whistled softly. "Well, whoever he is, he's good. Why can't all men be like that?"

From behind her, someone called out Max's name. Charley sucked in a breath. Had her heart stopped beating, too? Slowly, she turned, and as her gaze rested on his form, she exhaled a sigh.

Max looked better than ever in a navy blue jacket and matching trousers. His white, straight-collared shirt complimented his tanned skin. Naturally, he took the spotlight, and when he smiled at his friends, Charley's heart raced. Best of all, he arrived without a date. Amanda's plan must have worked.

He stood not more than ten feet away. Charley longed to walk over and talk to him, but the more she stared at him like a rock-star groupie, the more she lost her nerve. Just like in high school.

He moved away with his coworkers to the punch bowl and she grumbled under her breath. She'd missed her chance again!

Amanda nudged her arm and Charley glanced over her shoulder. Her supervisor nodded in Max's direction. "Go speak to him."

Charley scowled. "I can't. I wouldn't know what to say. It's not like we chat on a daily basis."

Amanda rolled her eyes. "You may not know him personally, but you know Fred and Gary. Act like you're going to talk to them."

Charley's throat tightened and she couldn't swallow. But what did she have to lose? If she didn't go over, she'd be upset with herself. If Max shot her down, at least she'd know he wasn't interested.

Besides, this wasn't high school anymore. The woman she'd turned into was more self-assured. Wasn't she?

She nodded to Amanda. "Wish me luck."

After taking a deep breath, Charley pulled back her shoulders and began her walk across the room, trying not to look like a coward.

Give him compliments. Tell him he looks nice. His hair does look good tonight.

When she drew near, Max's gaze seemed to resonate through her. He looked her over from the top of her wild hairdo to the toes of her shoes. She couldn't breathe. He looked into her eyes and smiled.

She felt like she would faint, but she couldn't. It would be embarrassing. Then again, if she did faint, he'd come pick her up and hold her in his strong arms. Since her lungs didn't work, he'd have to give her mouth-to-mouth resuscitation. The thought made her lightheaded.

Suddenly, her stomach lurched. *Please no! Not here. Not now. Not with Max watching.*

Before Charley knew what was happening, the room tilted and her legs gave out from underneath her. Her head connected with the floor like a bowling ball starting its run down to the pins. All sounds faded except for the ringing in her ears. Someone slipped an arm beneath her shoulders, lifted her, and lightly tapped her cheek.

She raised her heavy eyelids and focused on the person who held her. *Max! Wishes do come true.* She smiled.

Worry etched his brow. "Are you all right?" His voice reached through the bells chiming in her head.

She nodded, ignoring the pain shooting through her temples.

Give him compliments. Tell him he looks nice. His hair looks good.

"Max, thanks." She paused, trying to think of a compliment. "Um, did I ever tell you I think your butt has an intoxicating smile?"

That didn't sound right. Why weren't her mind and mouth cooperating tonight?

Max's eyes widened, and snickers sounded from the crowd who had gathered. Oh, no! Why hadn't she noticed the others?

Think! Charley had to say something to cover herself. "Um, I mean, your smile is outfitted in style. I mean, your butt looks stylish." She shook her head and inwardly groaned. "I think you really look good tonight."

Open mouth, insert foot. Heat flooded her cheeks, spreading quickly down her neck. The corner of Max's mouth lifted in a grin. She struggled to sit, but he tightened his hold.

"Charley, I think you hit your head pretty hard. You might want to rest a little before you stand up."

She squeezed her eyes tight. *Where's the nearest hole?* Maybe if she thought hard enough, she'd be back home and all this would be a bad dream. *This can't be happening.* Mentally, she tapped her heels together three times. *There's no place like home, there's no place like home.* Then she realized her heels were not ruby. And this for sure wasn't Kansas.

From the whispers around her, more people had gathered. Amanda's voice boomed loud and clear. "Here, Charley, drink this. You'll feel better."

Without opening her eyes, she reached blindly for the drink and curled her fingers around the glass stem. The chill of the flute soothed her hot skin. Another hand helped raise the glass to her lips, strong fingers guiding it to her mouth.

The arm behind her shoulders lifted her. Charley peeked underneath her lashes just as the glass touched her lips. The strong scent of alcohol assaulted her senses just as the liquid slid into her mouth.

She swallowed involuntarily. The liquid burned her throat, and she gagged and then gasped.

"I don't drink!" She clutched Max's arm.

"Oops," Amanda said, giving Charley an apologetic smile.

Charley cleared her throat and glanced at Max, who still looked at her in concern.

"Are you feeling better?"

She shook her head. "Now the burning in my throat is competing with the throbbing in my head."

His expression relaxed into a grin. "You've got your sense of humor back. That's good."

Her heart picked up rhythm. *He thinks I have a sense of humor? Cool!*

She looked around at the large crowd and groaned. Her hand massaged her temple. "I'll be fine in a minute."

"Here, let me help you over to the table."

The moment she'd dreamed about for weeks came when Max's arm slipped down her back and hooked around her waist. Hesitantly, she circled her arm around his neck, holding him close as he helped her off the floor. As soon as her feet touched the ground, her legs buckled and she stumbled into him, her face pressing into his neck.

Oh, he smells good—so incredibly male. So like Damien. Did they buy their cologne from the same place?

Max pushed her back slightly and helped her stand. Together, they walked to the nearest table, and he guided her onto a chair. He crouched beside her, his hands resting on her knee. Warmth spread from that spot. "How do you feel now?"

"A little better, thanks."

His gaze bore deep into her eyes. "Are you sure?"

She nodded.

"You still think my butt has an intoxicating smile?" He grinned.

She closed her eyes, covered her face with her hands, and groaned. Then, hearing Max chuckle, she peeked at him between her fingers.

"That's okay, Charley." His hands grasped hers and pulled them away from her face. "I appreciate the compliment no matter how it came out. I have to admit, nobody has ever said that to me before."

Through her embarrassment, she forced a smile. "Well, anytime you want to hear something out of the ordinary, you know where my cubicle is."

"Yes, I do." He laughed. "You know, I haven't seen a fall like that since the 1980 US Olympic Hockey team took the Cup."

"Oh, thanks. I feel so much better."

He stood. "Take it easy from here on out, okay?"

She nodded and watched him walk away. She felt almost giddy. *It's working!*

♡ Chapter Seven

Charley nibbled on another carrot. She leaned her hip against the buffet table then quickly pulled away before the table came crashing down. Her night had been full of blunders so far, and she didn't want to chance another one.

Out on the dance floor, smiling couples moved together with the rhythm of the music. Others wandered from group to group, talking and laughing. Everyone seemed to be having a good time. Everyone except her. Even Amanda had abandoned her. Charley's supervisor chatted with a group of editors on the other side of the room, batting her long eyelashes and laughing from time to time. Why couldn't she be cool like Amanda?

She turned her attention from Amanda's group and searched for Max. He was in another woman's arms, dancing in the middle of the ballroom. The bubbly blond who worked upstairs in sales rested her head on his shoulder, a wide, satisfied smile pasted to her face.

That should be me! Charley thought. But no, she had to embarrass herself and faint, just because he smiled at her.

I'm an idiot.

She reached for another glass of punch and sipped it. Max hadn't looked her way since he'd left her at the table. Perhaps she should faint again, just to have him come to her rescue.

She frowned. *How pathetic.*

Suddenly, she heard a baritone voice behind her.

"You're not going to catch men if your mouth is pulled into a frown, mi amore."

She gasped and spun around, almost spilling her drink down her dress. Her eyes nearly popped out of their sockets.

There stood Damien, wearing a dark suit jacket and trousers.

"What are you doing here?"

He shrugged. "Just passing by."

"Since when do you pass by this way?"

"Since I couldn't stop wondering how your evening was going."

Charley heaved a big sigh. "Not as well as I'd wanted." She looked over her shoulder at Max and the blond. "As you can see, he's over there and I'm here."

Damien leaned to the side, looking around her at Max. He chuckled. "Wow. They obviously put a lot of makeup on him so he can look good on TV."

She slugged his shoulder. "Be nice. You're insulting the next man in my life."

He frowned. "Sorry."

"So, really, Damien, what are you doing here?"

"It's like I said, I came to check on you, perhaps give you a little nudge in the right direction."

She shook her head. "You could shove me clear across the room and it wouldn't help."

"Have you talked to him?"

"Sort of."

His brown eyes widened. "And? What happened?"

"Instead of making him melt, he made *me* melt—all the way to the floor."

A smirk crossed Damien's face, and he quickly covered his mouth with his hand. "You don't say."

She slapped his shoulder again. "Be nice."

He nodded and dropped his hand from his mouth. "So what do you want me to do?"

She glanced at Max. "Well, since you're my fairy godfather, could you go sprinkle a little love dust on him?"

"I'll do one better." Slipping his arm around her waist, he pulled her close to him. "Let's make him jealous, shall we?"

"You?" She must have heard wrong. "I'm supposed to make him jealous with you?"

Damien scowled. "Don't you think I'm handsome enough?"

"Well, yes, but—"

"Then let's try, shall we?"

"What about . . . um . . . well, you know—" She paused. "What about your reputation?"

"What reputation?"

"Well, guys like you only go out with—"

"With?"

"With Barbie dolls."

He chuckled as he led her out to the dance floor. "Oh, they've got nothing on you, mi amore. Besides, you're my friend. I'd hate myself if I didn't at least try to help you."

She smiled and squeezed his arm. "Thanks, Damien. You're the best."

"Yes, I know."

When she tried to link her arms around his neck, he stopped her by taking one hand in his, letting the other hook over his shoulder. It surprised her to see him dance this way. This was how her parents used to dance. It was actually kind of nice. Although he looked like a bodybuilder, he danced with graceful ease, sweeping her around the floor. She hadn't danced this way since her mother taught her as a young girl. The more Damien swung her around like a professional ballroom dancer, the wider her smile grew.

She glanced over his broad shoulder as they passed Max. His eyes were wide, glued to her and Damien.

The song ended and a slower one began. Damien kept her in his arms in the same hold, but pulled her closer. She rested her cheek on his chest, breathing in his intoxicating scent. Max smelled this good too. Well, not quite as good, but close.

"Don't look now," Damien whispered, "but lover boy's watching."

She giggled. "Really?"

"Yes."

Charley raised her head and looked up at Damien. "So now what do we do?"

He leaned down and brushed his lips across her cheek. Goose bumps rose over her skin and she shivered, fighting the urge to close her eyes and tilt her head back.

"That tickles," she said softly.

"Keep still. It's working."

"Why?"

"Because he's coming this way."

Once again, her legs felt like JELL-O. Why couldn't she just pretend Max was Damien? After all, Damien was a great-looking guy. So why didn't she act like a squirming schoolgirl around him?

"Excuse me." Max's voice, so close behind her, made her catch her breath. She looked over her shoulder at him.

Damien stopped moving but kept his arms around her.

What a great friend, Charley thought. She smiled at Max. "Hi," she said in a soft voice.

Max looked even better than he had earlier. Of course, back then, her vision had been a little blurred because of her dizziness.

Max glanced from her to Damien. "Giovanni. It's been a long time."

Damien nodded. "Certainly has."

"Do you mind if I cut in?" Max motioned his head toward Charley. "I promised her a dance."

She looked at Damien, who didn't look as happy as he had a minute ago. His lips tightened and a crease appeared in his forehead.

"That's fine." He let go of her and walked away.

Max didn't pull her into the ballroom hold, but slid his arms around her waist instead. She linked her arms over his shoulders. Right away, she noticed the difference between the two men. Max, a little shorter, was also not as broad through the chest.

Max smiled as he gazed into her eyes, watching her carefully.

Heat rushed to her cheeks. *Is my hair messed up? Do I have carrot in my teeth?*

"How are you feeling?" Max began, the tone of his voice just as sweet as his smile.

"I'm much better, thank you. I don't know why I passed out earlier. Must have been hungry."

He nodded. "That'll happen."

She fell quiet again, as did he. The urge to speak nearly choked her, but nothing came to mind.

Max glanced over at the punch bowl where Damien stood, and she followed his gaze. Damien's somber stare remained on her, causing her heart to clench. *Why does he look so miserable?*

"How do you know Giovanni?" he asked.

"He's my neighbor."

"What a coincidence that you know him. We were friends in college."

She turned back to Max, opening her mouth to comment, then shutting it. He'd asked her to dance out of jealousy. How did Damien know Max would act this way?

"I didn't know that," she replied, hoping he wouldn't know she was lying through her teeth.

Max glanced at Damien. "How long have you been dating?"

Should she lie again? It was a sin to lie, but for some reason, she couldn't confess the truth. "Not for very long." *At least it wasn't a complete lie.*

"I see he hasn't lost his talent for sweeping the ladies around the dance floor."

"Really? He used to dance back then?"

"Yes." The arms around her waist tightened. "But you dance very well too."

"When I was a girl, my mother taught me how to do a few ballroom dances." She smiled in remembrance. "After the housework was finished on Saturdays, she'd pull out the records and crank up the volume. We'd dance right there in the front room."

Max chuckled with her.

"I remember being so embarrassed. I'd close the curtains so that if my friends walked by the house, they wouldn't see."

"You were an excellent student," he said.

"Thank you."

He was silent again. Why did he act this way? If she didn't know better, she'd think *he* was shy!

He cleared his throat. "I wanted to thank you for your email. I wondered about that plant."

She blushed. "I was so upset when I discovered that the wrong plant was sent. I wanted to tell you right away, but circumstances made it impossible. It was a rather busy day, wasn't it?"

"Yes."

"I hope no real damage was done."

He shook his head. "No, but your email explained why I'd gotten a rash and felt nauseated."

"I swear, I didn't know."

He nodded. "I'm aware of that, and I don't blame you."

She let out a heavy sigh. "That's a relief. I thought you'd blame me for the mix-up."

"No. I understand."

The music ended. Charley's chest grew heavy as she removed her arms from Max's neck. "Thanks for the dance," she said, hoping he'd ask for another.

"Thank you."

When he turned to walk away, she quickly touched his sleeve. "Hey, Max, are you here by yourself?"

He chuckled. "Although my date canceled at the last minute, I really wouldn't consider myself alone."

"Well, um, would you like to sit with me for a few minutes and have a drink?"

He glanced over her shoulder and then looked back at her. "I don't think Damien would appreciate that very much." He grinned and squeezed her hand. "But I'll catch up with you later."

"Promise?"

He nodded and then turned and walked back to his friends.

Later! He's going to find me later. But her enthusiasm lessened when she remembered he'd only danced with her because he was jealous. Should she really let him think she was dating Damien? If she did, would Max give up? Funny, the Internet article didn't mention anything about making a man jealous.

"Another drink, please."

Damien scowled at Charley as she sat with hunched shoulders at the bar. Thankfully, she only sipped on fruit punch drink rather than champagne. Then again, she had been acting funny. Had someone spiked the punch? Her mood had turned sour quickly, yet her personality seemed almost, well, dopey.

"Charley, I think it's time to take you home. You don't look too good." Not only was she dressed to kill, she now staggered into people like a runaway train.

"Damien, leave me alone," she slurred, pushing his hand away. "I'm waitin' for Max to come rescue me."

"Come on, honey. Let's go."

"No." She glared at him. "He promised to dance with me again."

Damien sighed. "I think Max has already left."

She turned her head so quickly that she lost her balance and started sliding off the barstool. Damien caught her around the waist and held her straight.

"Really?" She looked at him sadly.

"Yes, mi amore, really. I saw him leave half an hour ago."

Her brows drew together. "What was I doin'?"

"You were probably drinking another glass of fruit punch."

She glanced back at the bartender, who nodded.

"Well, that's a grand idea," she said loudly. "Drinks for everyone." She held up her empty glass and would have fallen backward if Damien hadn't been holding her up.

"Good grief, Charley. Have you been drinking something other than punch?"

"'Course not. I never drink alcohol. I told you that."

"Then why are you acting drunk?"

95

"I'm not drunk." She waved her hand through the air, nearly hitting his head. "Although," she met his gaze, "I've been feeling funny since I took the pills you gave me."

He groaned. The decongestant was obviously too strong for her. "Come on, then. It's definitely time to get you home and put you in bed." He pried the glass from her hand and passed it to the bartender.

She huffed. "You're no fun."

As they left the party, Charley called out goodbyes to her coworkers, who looked at her with wide eyes. Damien hoped she wouldn't get teased at work on Monday.

When they reached the parking lot, he helped her to his black Porsche and buckled her in the seat. Her body went limp, but when he climbed in the driver's seat, she giggled and reached for his arm, cuddling up next to him.

"Did you see the way Max danced with me, Damien?"

"Yes." He had watched every second of the time she had spent in Max's arms, and at the time he'd wanted to go break up the cozy moment. *He* wanted to be the man holding the beautiful woman. *He* wanted to be the man Charley gazed up at so lovingly.

"Max isn't as good a dancer as you, but he still knew how to move." She sighed. "He's certainly a handsome man."

Damien balled his hands into fists. "If you say so."

He moved her aside to adjust his seatbelt, and she rolled her head on the headrest and looked at him.

"You really need to find someone special, you know that, Damien?"

"Yes, Charley." Finding someone special—now that was a talent he'd never possessed. "Someone to have a good time with" fit his lifestyle much better. Yet lately he'd been tired of his carefree ways, and he'd been thinking that Charley was a *very* special woman.

She brought out the best in him, and he liked it. She made him think of going back to church, which is something he never thought he'd do. Funny that this good little Mormon girl could make him want to become the kind of man she would date.

"It's not good to go from one woman to another," she continued. "You need that special someone to love— forever."

He met her gaze, then looked down at her pouty lips. What would she do if he kissed her right now?

He couldn't. He wouldn't!

Diverting his stare, he looked out the windshield and started the car, then pulled out of the nearly empty parking lot, the heat of her gaze still on him.

"Damien?" Her voice sounded husky.

"Yes?"

"Have you ever kissed one of your friends before?"

He glanced at her. "Of course not. I'm not that kind of guy."

Charley scrunched her forehead, but after a few seconds she giggled. "No, I didn't mean your guy friends. I meant the women you consider your friends."

His heart hammered and his throat tightened. *What is she getting at?* "Yes. I've kissed you before, or have you forgotten?"

She flipped her hand through the air. "Not that kind of a kiss. I mean a passionate kiss."

Damien tried to focus on the road. She didn't know how much he wanted to do that very thing. He wanted to kiss her—kiss her until he was the only man in her head and in her heart.

"Charley, just close your eyes and relax. We'll be home shortly."

"Damien," she whined, "why are you avoidin' my question?"

He gripped the steering wheel tighter. "Because I don't see the point in discussing this."

"Are you embarrassed?"

"No, not as embarrassed as you're going to be if you keep it up."

"Damien." She poked him in the side and he jumped. "You can talk to me about anythin', you know."

"I know."

She jabbed her finger in his side once again, but this time he didn't jump. Her hand moved to his arm and stayed. Automatically, he covered her hand with his and squeezed. As he pressed harder on the gas pedal, one thought filled his mind: getting her home as fast as he could, before he pulled over and took her in his arms.

"Then why don't you want to talk to me?"

"What do you want me to talk about?"

"I want to know about you and Max."

"I don't feel like discussing him."

"Do you want to talk about why you don't go to church anymore?"

"No."

Her fingers rubbed his sleeve, and he masked a groan by clearing his throat.

"I think you should. The Lord will forgive you, and He will take you back with open arms. Heavenly Father wants you to return to Him. In fact, if you would like, you could come to church with me."

A lump formed in Damien's throat. He wondered how long it had been since he'd prayed, how long since he'd believed God actually answered prayers. *Maybe,* Damien thought, *I still blame God for what's happened in my life.*

Curling his fingers around Charley's, he moved her hand from his arm. She sighed and he glanced at her. A sweet smile touched her lips, and her eyes were closed. She must be thinking about Max.

When he drove up to the townhouse complex, he breathed a sigh of relief, thinking she'd fallen asleep. But when he pulled her out of the car and lifted her off her feet, she wrapped her arms around his neck and buried her face in his chest.

"Hmm . . . you smell so good," she mumbled.

He carried her until they reached her townhouse, then leaned her against the wall as he searched through her purse for her keys. After opening the door, he shifted Charley in his arms and carried her to her bedroom.

He sat her on the edge of the bed and gently removed her coat. Then she flung herself back and sprawled out on the pink comforter, resting her arms above her head. A smile still spread across her mouth, her eyes closed as if in a dream. Should he throw a blanket over her and leave? He just couldn't stop looking at her, wishing for something he would never have.

In the front room he found a blanket flung over the back of the couch, so he brought it back into the bedroom and gently covered Charley with it. He stared at her for a moment, wishing he could confess his true feelings. Spending time with her lately had put a spark back in his life—had somehow given it direction. Most of his friends had given up asking him why he'd stopped going to church. It touched his heart that Charley cared. But he couldn't say anything to her, not yet. He'd wait to see what happened between her and Max first. There was no way he wanted to compete with Max again.

Before he left, Damien bent and kissed her forehead. Her body jerked and her eyes flew open.

He smiled and stroked his finger along her jaw. "Pleasant dreams, mi amore."

She grasped his hand. "Don't leave me."

He shook his head. "Honey, you're home in bed. It's all right."

"No. I don't want to be alone. Can't you stay and talk?"

He sat on the edge of the bed and lifted her hand to his mouth, kissing her knuckles. "You're in no condition to talk right now, my love. The pills have pretty much knocked you out. It's best if you rest."

"But I like having you here."

"Charley, I've got to go home."

With his other hand, he trailed his fingertips over her cheek. Her gaze dropped to his mouth and his heart beat an uneven rhythm. He traced her lips and they parted, her fragrant breath touching his skin.

She turned and propped herself up on her elbow, then pulled Damien's hand to her mouth and kissed it. Did she know what she was doing?

"Charley—"

She shook her head. "I know you want to kiss me."

Obviously, she could read his mind well. But would she ever consider him good enough to date, to fall in love with?

He kept his gaze on hers as he leaned forward. As he neared, she closed her eyes, her lips puckering slightly. When he placed his mouth over hers for a soft kiss, she sighed and leaned into him. She pushed her fingers through his hair as she kissed him.

He took things slowly, knowing he didn't want to treat her like his past girlfriends. Charley was too special. She had higher standards, and he didn't want her to lower them for him. He didn't think he could ever reach her level, but he wanted to try, and if that meant going to church with her, he would. He craved her respect like a thirsty man craved water. And, as amazing as it sounded, he hungered for the Lord's guidance in his life again.

Damien didn't want to think of why she would kiss him, or

wonder if she'd regret it in the morning. For now, he wanted to let her know, through his kiss, how much she meant to him.

When he reluctantly pulled his lips from hers, Damien stroked his thumbs across her cheeks. Her eyes fluttered open, and she appeared to be half asleep. A smile curved her lips and his heart soared.

As he leaned in for another kiss, she mumbled a name under her breath and he stopped.

Max? Did she just say *Max?*

Of course she thought he was Max! Max was the man Charley wanted, not Damien.

He pulled away from her and let her body fall to the mattress. Finally, she'd drifted into dreamland. He moved off the bed and pulled the blanket over her.

As he left her townhouse, Damien's heart grew heavy. If she thought she'd been kissing Max, he wouldn't embarrass her by telling her otherwise.

♡Chapter Eight

Intense throbbing in Charley's head roused her from a deep sleep. She didn't have to open her eyes to know the sun shone a brilliant path through her window onto her face. She groaned and clutched the edge of her pillow, rolling away from the light. That helped a bit but the pounding still raged. From the back of her mind came a nagging feeling that she'd done something wrong.

Through her fierce headache she recalled the party, the dance with Max, and . . . Damien. Thank goodness for Damien, always there to take care of her.

Then, in a flash, she remembered. She sat upright, opening her eyes. Her stomach lurched and she yanked back the blanket and ran to the bathroom, making it just in time to vomit into the toilet.

She clutched her head, then her stomach, and then tried holding them both. Had she heaved up every organ in her body?

She grabbed a hand towel and pressed it to her mouth. Slowly, she stood, her legs as wobbly as a newborn calf's. The pounding in her head increased, but at least her stomach had calmed. She rinsed her mouth out at the sink, then weaved her way back into the bedroom to lie face first on the bed.

What had she done? Had she really kissed Damien?

Yes, her blurry memories told her. And Damien had *let* her kiss him, knowing she thought he was Max. Why?

With a groan, Charley climbed underneath the covers and curled into a ball. *I kissed my neighbor, someone I have no romantic feelings for! Great.*

She remembered the way Damien's hands had stroked her cheek, the way his mouth had moved on hers, and especially the way she'd felt in his arms. He'd been so gentle and so sweet. But why hadn't he just left? He knew what condition she was in because of the decongestant. Maybe their friendship meant nothing to him. Maybe he'd been drinking last night and that was why he'd kissed her. She couldn't think of another explanation. Yet Damien had never drunk alcohol around her, and as far as she knew he didn't drink at all.

She pulled her knees to her chest. Would he ever speak to her again? Would this ruin their friendship? Most importantly, had he enjoyed kissing her as much as she had him—enough to want to change into the religious man she wanted?

She shook her head fiercely. The thought of Damien going to church on Sunday was ridiculous. There was no way he would even consider it. And if Charley hadn't changed any of her boyfriends—and she hadn't—why did she think she could change him? The more she thought about her failed relationships, the more her head throbbed. She needed to get up and eat some crackers or something, but just thinking about food turned her stomach.

Once again, her thoughts wandered back to the previous evening. She simply could not recall how Damien had looked after he kissed her. In fact there were a lot of things she couldn't remember. Perhaps she'd dreamed all of it.

The pounding in her head grew until it sounded like the walls were crashing together. Or was somebody at her front door? She pulled the pillow closer to her ears, hoping whoever it was would go away and take that noise with them.

She heard movement in her living room. She listened closer. Had someone broken in?

"Charley?"

She sighed heavily. It was Damien. As his footsteps drew nearer, she pulled the blankets up to her chin, even though she still had on the gown from last night.

Damien knocked on the bedroom door before he peeked in and smiled at her. "So, you are awake."

"Barely." Her voice squeaked.

He held up a glass filled with red foamy liquid. "I hope you don't mind, but I used your keys to open the door. I've brought something for your head cold." He walked into the room.

"What is it?"

"A concoction to make your recovery smoother from the pill I gave you last night."

"Did you make this?"

"Yes. It's a family secret that's been passed down through the generations."

"I take it you've had a lot of sick people in your family."

He chuckled and stepped close to the bed. "Do you want it or not? I promise within an hour you'll feel much better."

She nodded and sat, letting the covers fall to her waist. He sat on the edge of the bed and tilted the glass to her mouth. She placed a shaky hand over his and guided the drink to her lips. The foam rose instead of heading down her throat, and she gagged and pushed the drink away. "Yuck."

He laughed. "It's not the best tasting, but it will help. Drink all of it."

She grimaced and shook her head. "I don't want to throw up all over you."

"You won't."

She held up her hand. "Please, no more. I'd rather have a congested headache."

"Suit yourself."

An uncomfortable silence followed, and Charley looked into Damien's eyes. The look she saw there bothered her, especially when he kept staring at her as if trying to read her thoughts. *She didn't even understand the confusion swimming in her head, so how could he?*

Damien glanced around the room, then back at her. "So, how was your evening with Max last night?"

A breath caught in Charley's throat. Why did he think she'd been with Max last night?

Her head pounded. "Max wasn't here."

"Yes, he was. He was with you last night."

Her head pounded. Had Max been the one to bring her home? Had it been Max she'd kissed so tenderly instead of Damien? Her stomach churned. Oh, how she wished she could remember! Damien said she was with Max last night, and why would he lie?

"Damien, don't play games with me. I don't remember being with Max last night, except at the party."

"Really?" Damien looked genuinely surprised.

Charley frowned. Her memories must have been wrong, or maybe she had dreamed the whole thing. But why did it seem so real? Why could she almost feel Damien's hands on her cheeks, his lips on hers?

"Well, I was pretty goofy last night because of those pills," she finally admitted. "Anything could have happened."

He chuckled and stood. "True." He placed the drink on the

stand next to her bed. "Well, I'll leave this here if you change your mind. I've got to get to work." Leaning over, Damien kissed her forehead. "Aren't you glad today is Saturday?"

She nodded. "You'll never know how blessed I feel. Monday will be hard enough, with people at work asking me questions and maybe even laughing at me"

"Okay, well, see you." Damien winked, then turned and walked out. With a frustrated sigh, Charley slammed her fist into the mattress.

When he walked out of the elevator and headed toward his office, Damien gave a polite nod to the people who greeted him. The lab technicians at GIO had been working on a new product, but Damien didn't care right now. All he could think about was the night before with Charley. He couldn't get the image of her out of his mind. He couldn't stop thinking about the way she'd returned his kiss, and the way she'd felt in his arms.

He also couldn't stop thinking about the name he thought he'd heard her sighing. Mistake or not, she'd been thinking about Max.

Yet according to her statement this morning, she didn't think she'd spent time with Max after the party. So why had she sighed his name? Damien would give anything to hear Charley whisper *his* name like that.

Could he have heard wrong? He doubted it.

He walked into his office and closed the door. Just as he made it to his desk, the office door opened.

"Damieno?" His mother's tone was sweet and caring. "There are a million things we need to do, and don't forget about the board meeting with our investors today at three."

He chuckled. "Which explains why you won't give me two minutes to myself this morning."

She walked to him with her hands on her hips. "You haven't been focused lately, so you need me now more than ever before."

He stood and kissed her cheek. "It's good to see you care, Mother."

As she smiled, her brown eyes sparkled. "What a charmer you are."

He laughed. "Did Michelle get those documents to you?"

"Yes. She brought them by the house two days ago."

"Good. I'd hate to think I was paying her good money for nothing."

"Stop talking about your baby sister like that. She's a hard worker and you know it."

He raised an eyebrow. "She's only a hard worker if her goal is flirting with single young men."

His mother flipped her hand in the air. "What do you expect from a nineteen-year-old? In fact, why aren't you trying to catch somebody's eye?"

"Too busy." He sat in his brown leather chair and opened his briefcase.

"That's not what I heard."

"What did you hear, Mother?" he asked without looking at her. For years now, stories had circulated around the office. Most were untrue, but they were certainly entertaining.

"I heard you've been hitting on your neighbor."

He looked up at her.

"Is this true?" she asked with a broad smile.

"Who told you that?"

"Your sister. She said you were all dressed up last night just to help out your neighbor at her office Christmas party. She said you seemed so different—so happy—and that you didn't use foul language around her like you used to. She said you even treated her with respect."

Damien let out an uneasy laugh. "Michelle is making up stories again."

Bella narrowed her eyes. "So you're saying you don't have a neighbor?"

This was all he needed—for his mother to know he had a crush on a girl before he knew if anything would even come of it. "I do have a neighbor who happens to be a woman, but she's just a friend." He shrugged and removed some papers from his briefcase. "She thinks of me as her friend. That's all."

His mother let out an exasperated breath and slapped her hands on his desk. He looked up and raised his eyebrows. "Damieno, you've been lying to another woman, haven't you?"

"Mother—"

"Why haven't you told her the truth?"

"I've told you before. I'm protecting myself from fortune hunters."

"You're also throwing away your social life."

"I have a social life."

Bella arched a brow. "Sure, with women who think of you only as their best friend. Now tell me, what kind of life is that?"

"It's a life with no heartaches, that's what it is."

"You can't let one heartache control your whole life, my dear son. The Lord has someone special in mind for you. I believe it, and I wish you would as well."

He took a deep breath and slowly counted to ten. "Mother, you're meddling again."

"But Damieno, I just want you to be happy." She squeezed his hand. "You'll be thirty-one in two months. Don't you think it's time you settled down and raised a family?"

"I do, but I'll settle down on my own time, and the children will come when I'm ready for them, and not a moment sooner."

She stood straight and folded her arms across her chest. "You're upset with me again."

He exhaled slowly and ran his fingers through his hair. "No, I just wish you'd stop lecturing me. I've heard this speech before. I know what I need to do."

She nodded, then turned and walked back to the door. When her hand touched the knob, she glanced over her shoulder. "Oh, and speaking of fortune hunters, Liza Scapolli is back in town."

The name struck him like a hammer, bringing back unwanted memories. It'd happened seven years ago. Why was the anger as fresh as if it'd happened last week?

His mother walked out of the office before he could ask why Liza was back in town. But he really didn't care what Liza and Max had done to him. At least he didn't *want* to care.

♡Chapter Nine

Charley kept her eyes downcast as she hurried through the front doors at Channel Nine. As she rushed by, she glanced at her coworkers out of the corner of her eye, but thankfully none of them looked at her as if she'd grown two heads.

When she reached her cubicle, she slid into her chair. It rocked to one side and tilted. She nearly plowed face first into her desk, but she grabbed the edge and steadied herself. *Phew!* She peeked out from beneath lowered lashes. No eyes had turned her way, and she heaved a sigh of relief.

Resting her elbows on the desk, Charley leaned her face into her hands and massaged her forehead. Yesterday at church she'd tried to listen to the talks and lessons, but Damien and Max had occupied most of her thoughts. Actually, *Damien* had occupied most of her thoughts! Since the night of her attack when he had rescued her, she had thought of him in a different light, and little by little she'd let him into her heart. Would the Lord be displeased with her if she decided Damien was the man she wanted, even if he didn't attend church?

She shook away the thought. Of course He would be displeased, and so would she. For most of her life, she'd dreamed of and planned for a temple marriage, and she wouldn't settle for anything less. Until Damien showed signs of wanting to come back to the Church, she couldn't allow him into her heart.

Within minutes, other workers entered the building. Like every other Monday, they dragged themselves to their desks. All except one employee. Max. When he finally arrived, he practically bounced down the hallway, and his smile could have melted an iceberg.

Charley gasped as he looked right at her, raised his hand, and waggled his fingers.

In shock, she tried to smile, and somehow she managed to return Max's wave. He chuckled as he headed toward his office.

What was that all about? She was almost afraid to ask. Why had he looked at her that way? Unless . . .

Charley caught her breath and almost choked. Had Max taken her home the night of the party and been the one to kiss her? That's what Damien had said. She needed to talk to Amanda.

After the morning news rush, the office buzzed. The employees of Channel Nine had left their desks and seemed more concerned with socializing than with work. Some gathered inside cubicles, and others wandered outside for a break. It wasn't hard to find Amanda, who stood, as usual, in the middle of a group of men.

Charley hurried over and yanked on her elbow. When Amanda turned, her eyes went wide. "Charley."

Charley glanced down to make sure she wasn't still wearing her pajamas. No, she was dressed in a conservative white blouse and gray slacks. Then she reached up and touched the side of her hair, tucking a stray lock behind her ear. Everything seemed to be in order. So why did Amanda and a few of the others gathered around look at her that way?

111

She met Amanda's stare. "We need to talk."

Amanda excused herself and kept in step beside Charley as they walked to her desk. Once they were out of earshot of the others, Amanda giggled.

"Charley, you're the talk of the office today. Everybody's discussing the Christmas party, and especially you."

Charley's heart sank as she wondered what they were saying.

Amanda clasped Charley's hands. "Are you going to tell me every juicy detail about Friday night?"

Charley scratched her head. "I was rather hoping you could tell me the details."

Amanda's brows lifted and she let out a loud laugh. "Oh, you're funny. Why do you think I'd be able to tell you?"

"You were there, weren't you?"

Her friend looked at her quizzically. "Charley, I don't think we're talking about the same thing here."

Charley took a deep breath, trying to clear her head. "I want to know what happened at the party."

Amanda laughed. "Oh, let me guess. After tasting your first champagne, you realized you had to have more, then got drunk?"

"I wasn't drunk! I had taken a decongestant before coming to the party. I think that's what made me act so loopy."

Amanda shrugged. "If you say so. What do you want to know?"

"I want to know whom I left the party with."

Amanda tipped back her head and laughed so hard that tears came to her eyes. Charley gritted her teeth. This was *not* a laughing matter. Her memory was at stake here, and the truth could either make or break her. If she didn't find out who'd kissed her so tenderly, she'd go crazy.

Finally, Amanda gained control of herself and said, "Sorry, but I don't know who you left the party with. I left before you did."

"Really?" Charley sighed.

"So, you don't remember anything?"

"I recall some things, but as the evening dragged on, my memory becomes fuzzy."

"Oh, I wish I could have been a fly on your wall that night."

"What night?" a male voice asked.

Charley jumped and swung around. Max! How long had he been standing there?

He leaned his elbow on the corner of her cubicle, his gaze moving over her as if she were a dessert menu. When his blue eyes met hers again, his smile grew.

"What night?" he repeated.

Charley released an uneasy laugh and flipped her hand in the air, her fingers accidentally connecting with Amanda's face. Her supervisor yelped and stepped back, holding her nose.

Charley cringed. "Oh, Amanda, I'm sorry."

"No problem," Amanda mumbled from behind her hand. "I'll be back in a minute." Then Amanda hurried down the hall toward the restrooms.

Max laughed. "Way to go, Charley. If you wanted a private moment with me, all you had to do was ask her to leave."

What is that *supposed to mean?* Charley thought.

His expression softened. "So, about Friday night—"

She swallowed hard. "What about it?"

"I think I should apologize."

"Why? Didn't you, um, enjoy yourself?"

He nodded. "I did, but I don't think you did."

"Of course I did." Charley forced a laugh. "Why would you think differently?"

"Well, considering all the alcohol you drank—"

Why does everything think I was drunk? Her hands started to tremble, so she sat on the edge of her desk and folded her arms to keep them still. "Actually, I don't drink alcohol. The reason I acted strangely that night was because of the decongestant I took before coming to the party."

"Decongestant?" Max dropped his arm from the corner of the cubicle and stepped closer. "I don't know anyone who's had such a reaction to a cold pill."

"Now you do. Ever since I was in junior high, decongestants have made me loopy." She shrugged. "I gave quite a show, if I recall correctly."

"Yes." He stroked the side of her face with his finger. "You did give quite a show and said some amazing things."

"Did, um, would . . ." She took a deep breath, trying to gather her wits. "Would you like to see a repeat performance?" *Now why did I say that?* She scolded herself, wishing she would think before she spoke.

His eyebrows rose. "Are you asking me out, Charley?"

She gulped. "I—I suppose I am."

"What about your heartthrob, Giovanni?"

She raised a shoulder. "We're more like good friends."

"I see." Max smiled. "Then my answer is yes."

Her heart leapt to her throat. "Great."

"Is the dance included in our date?"

He wants to go dancing with me? "Um, okay."

"How about dinner first?"

She thought back to the article on how to win a man. Number 4 was an old-fashioned date. She nodded and smiled. "Dinner first, but I'm cooking."

He grinned broadly. "You sure are."

She blushed and the room seemed to close in around her,

making it difficult to breathe. "No, I mean, we'll have dinner at my house."

He nodded. "How about tomorrow night?"

"Sounds good. Does seven o'clock work?"

"Works for me."

He leaned forward and she held her breath. Was he going to kiss her right there in front of everyone? Thank goodness he withdrew before she had a chance to pucker up.

He turned and strode confidently to his office. Charley moved from the corner of her desk to her chair, then stared at the dark computer screen. In her reflection, she wore a smile. As her mind finally began to work, she realized Max had never said he took her home that night. He'd hinted at it, but he never actually came out and said it.

What could she make him for dinner? She groaned and rubbed her forehead. She wasn't a chef; that was Damien's specialty. He was always cooking up something special for his women friends. She could smell the food from her townhouse all the time.

She snatched up the phone, quickly punching in Damien's cell number. Drumming her fingers on the desktop, she let it ring four times and was about to hang up when he answered.

"Hello?"

She sighed. "Oh, Damien, I'm glad you're there."

"Charley? What's wrong?"

"Nothing's wrong. In fact, everything is right." She giggled and relaxed back in her swivel chair, twirling the phone cord around her finger. "You'll never guess who's coming to my house for dinner tomorrow."

There was a long pause. "Me?"

She sucked in her breath. Had she detected a sense of hopefulness in his voice?

"No, silly. Max is coming. Oh, Damien, I actually carried on a normal discussion with him and nobody got hurt. Can you believe it?"

"No," he answered quietly.

"Yeah, me neither." She giggled. "Actually, I did smack Amanda in the nose while Max was talking to me, but that doesn't count."

"So, what are you planning to fix, TV dinners?"

"Ha, ha, very funny. But you're also very right. That's all I ever eat. Anyway, I need your help. In the Internet article, number 4 says I have to give him an old-fashioned date. So, I want to cook him a meal." She paused briefly. "I mean, what could be more old fashioned than that?"

"How about snaring a jackrabbit and cooking it over a fire?"

A hint of sarcasm laced Damien's voice, and Charley hoped she'd heard wrong. "Does that mean you won't help me?"

A long period of silence followed, and with each second, her heart sank. He didn't want to help, but she couldn't do it without him.

Finally, a heavy sigh came across the line and he cleared his throat. "Yes, Charley, I'll help you. I'll do anything for you. You know that."

"Oh, Damien, you're a lifesaver." If he were standing in front of her now, she'd throw her arms around him and bury her face in his neck . . .

"Yes, I know," he said with a catch in his voice.

She wanted to rush to his side, to see his face and know how he felt. Instead, she said, "Thanks, Damien. I'll love you forever for this, you know. What would I do without you?"

"I hope I never find out."

Damien clutched his briefcase and stormed out of his shareholders' meeting, straight toward his office. GIO Products was looking for a female model for a new promotion, and women filled the lobby from wall to wall. He dodged around those who tried to stop him to get an introduction.

When he passed his secretary, she held up a hand to stop him. He ignored her and hurried inside his office, closing the door behind him. He needed some privacy.

He set his briefcase on the desk and walked to the wide window that overlooked the city. As he gazed at the busy traffic, he pinched the bridge of his nose and breathed deeply. From the 90-minute meeting with shareholders, Damien only remembered six words: "Good morning" and "Have a nice day."

Why couldn't he stop thinking about Charley? And why had he agreed to help her fix dinner for the date she would have with Max, not him? Well, he was a man of his word, though the dinner just wouldn't be what she expected. It might be a little vindictive, but he wanted Charley for himself, and that meant getting rid of Max—only figuratively, of course.

So far, Max hadn't given any signs of changing his ways. The man Damien knew in college went after women who belonged to others, and Charley's office party had proven Max was still up to his old tricks. Max had responded perfectly to the jealousy setup, going after Charley when it appeared she was seeing someone. What would stop the sports anchorman from going after the next attractive conquest he saw?

Damien walked to his swivel chair and dropped into it. Out the window, the tall building blocked his view of the nearby park. From what he could see, the blue sky held only a few clouds, but a storm was moving into town. And by the way the limbs on the trees waved, the storm would be here quicker than he expected. He'd always liked wintertime; cold weather was perfect for

Marie Higgins

cuddling with a woman near a roaring fire.

He smiled and pictured himself and Charley sitting together in front of a fireplace. It could happen. Although he didn't have a fireplace in his townhouse, his cabin in Colorado had three. It'd been a while since he'd been there. Perhaps it was time to take Charley and show her how the real Damien Giovanni lived.

The knock on his office door jolted him out of his daydreams. The door opened a crack and his secretary, Mary Ann, peeked her head inside.

"Mr. Giovanni? There's someone here to see you."

He glanced down at the day's schedule in his day planner. "I didn't forget an appointment, did I?"

"No. She's been waiting since right after your meeting started."

He frowned. "Who is it?"

Mary Ann hurried to his desk and handed him a business card. "Says she's the vice president of Herbal Sensations."

Their competitors. "Really?" He glanced down at the card. As his gaze skimmed the name, Mary Ann spoke the words aloud.

"Her name is Liza Scapolli."

118

Chapter Ten ♡

Damien drummed his fingers on his desk and clenched his jaw. He'd just told his secretary to allow *that woman* into his office. What was he thinking? He'd gone seven years without talking to her, and he knew he could go another seven—or seventy—and be just fine.

When he dated Liza, Damien had thought she was the woman for him. He had prayed about her and hoped things could work out, but he hadn't really seen who she was until it was too late.

Once he married her and realized his mistake, he'd turned to the Lord, begging for a way out of the situation. But the Lord didn't save him, and Damien became bitter. Looking back, Damien now realized his flawed thinking. He'd chosen to marry Liza without waiting for the Lord's blessing, and then he'd had to deal with the awful consequences. Damien had turned from the Lord and His true Church—all because things didn't go as Damien had hoped. He'd been so angry at Heavenly Father for deserting him. Now he realized that he had blamed God for his problems and then deserted Him.

The clicking of heels outside Damien's door caused him to glare in that direction. He fisted his hands on the desktop, crinkling the paper beneath. Realizing he'd smashed an important document, he smoothed out the wrinkles, then placed it on the desk out of his way.

The door opened and Damien saw the Italian woman who'd trampled his heart. She'd been his first love but thankfully not his last. What was the backstabbing woman up to now?

Liza Scapolli pushed her sunglasses to the top of her head. Long, black hair cascaded down her shoulders, and the smile she wore looked as fake as her leather miniskirt.

"Damieno, my dear. How long has it been?"

He lifted his eyebrows in what he hoped would be an unexpressive look. "Obviously, not long enough."

She shut the door and sauntered over to him. Instead of sitting on one of the brown leather chairs in front of his desk, she sat on the edge of his desk, crumpling the document he'd previously unwrinkled.

Leaning back in his chair, Damien linked his fingers over his stomach. "To what do I owe the pleasure, Liza?"

She crossed one leg over the other, batting her heavily mascaraed eyelashes. "Since I was in the neighborhood, I thought I'd come and say hello."

"Fine. Now that you've said hello, you can leave. I'm very busy today."

She pouted. "Too busy for a friend?"

He sat up. "Friend?" He looked beyond her as if someone else were in the room. "My friend is here? Where?"

"Oh, Damieno, you haven't lost your sense of humor."

"I am very busy. If you haven't noticed, the lobby is packed with women waiting to audition. So, Liza, please say what you've come to say and leave."

She gasped and quickly stood. "I'm appalled you don't believe I'm here for a little visit. Perhaps I should leave and come back when you're in better spirits."

He rolled his eyes. "Liza, I know you better than to think you've come to see me just because you've missed me. In fact, I'm willing to bet you're here because your attempts to start production in Colorado fell through, and now you've come back to California to talk me into becoming your partner."

Her eyes widened and she placed her hand over her heart. "Why would you think such a thing?"

"I'd heard you were back in town, so I checked out your company. I think Herbal Sensations is worried about GIO's new herbal lines. In fact, all the analysts agree our products are better. Since you stole the idea from me in the first place, I'm thinking you need my help. I believe you want to form an alliance."

Even through her caked-on makeup, Liza's skin lost a little color. She stared at Damien with her dark eyes, still smiling. He was right. The little heathen was still performing. Seven years ago he'd thought the sun rose just to shine on her every morning, but he was over her now! Still, he deeply resented the fact that she'd entered his life again. This could only mean problems.

Finally, her lips fell into a scowl. She took a step back and plopped into a chair on the other side of his desk. "Damieno, you're being very unreasonable."

He snickered. "I have every right to be unreasonable. Seven years ago you said you loved me, just to get information. Didn't you think I'd catch on? Not even four months after you left, I heard of a new company selling herbal shampoo, and guess who is vice president and married to the president? None other than my ex."

Liza's delicate eyebrows furrowed. "That's not how it happened and you know it. Besides, I'm not with Dale any longer.

I never got over my feelings for you. I loved you—"

"And that's why you made the moves on my best friend?"

"It's not what you think. Maxwell Harrington was just comforting me—"

He held up a hand. "It doesn't matter now. You have your company and I have mine." He smiled. "And my company is doing so much better than it was while we were together."

Liza glanced at her hands as she twisted them against her stomach. "Damieno, don't you even want to hear my offer?" Her voice was low.

"Not really."

She gave him a venomous look, and a muscle in her cheek jumped. "And why not?" she asked.

"Because I don't need you."

She leaned forward. "But, Damieno, think how much more money your company could make. There's nothing wrong with Herbal Sensations. We just need stronger backing."

He pushed away from his desk. "Sorry, Liza, but I'm not interested." He moved closer to her. "I'm not interested in anything you have to offer."

"But your mother seemed pleased with the idea."

"My mother doesn't know you're a bloodthirsty shark."

Liza huffed. "You're a very stubborn man."

"True, but I think you're more upset because you haven't been able to sink your claws into me this time."

"Oh!" She pushed her palms against his chest and walked past him. Her heels clicked loudly on the floor as she stomped out the door, then slammed it shut behind her.

He breathed a sigh of relief, but he knew she'd be back.

An old-fashioned night on the town

The next day, as Damien stood in front of his townhouse unlocking the door, Charley came flying out of her front door.

"Damien, you're late," she said breathlessly.

He glanced down at his watch. "Only by ten minutes."

"We have to hurry! Max will be here in two hours."

Damien chuckled and opened his door, motioning for Charley to enter first. When she stepped past him, he breathed in her scent.

"We have plenty of time, mi amore."

"Have you thought of what we could fix for dinner?"

He shut the door behind him and leaned against the wood. "No, have you?"

She nodded. "I thought about some exotic French dish."

"Oh, that's good."

Her smile brightened. "Really?"

"Yes. I have everything we need in my kitchen." He moved away from the door and in three steps stood in front of her. "I have French dressing to go on the tossed green salad. I have French fries that will go great with French bread."

She slapped his shoulder and laughed. "Be serious."

"Okay, I'll be serious, but just for tonight." He paused in thought. "I have it. We'll fix my specialty, cinnamon chicken and cheesy scalloped potatoes."

"Hmm. Sounds heavenly." She rubbed her hands together. "And what about a vegetable?"

"Would you rather have asparagus or broccoli?"

She scrunched her nose. "Definitely not asparagus."

He winked. "Then broccoli it is." He clasped her hand and hooked it around his elbow. "Now, cherie, if you'll allow me to escort you into zee kitchen, ve'll prepare zee most tastiest dish that's ever touched your tongue," he said in a bad French accent.

She laughed as Damien led her to the kitchen sink. "Since I have everything we need, we'll just prepare it here."

She nodded. "But I want it to cook in my kitchen. My place needs to smell like I've been laboring over a hot stove."

He dug through a drawer full of recipes and pulled one out. Charley leaned near him, peering at the card.

"You get the chicken, and I'll grab the other ingredients," she said.

"Sounds like a plan."

He moved to the refrigerator and retrieved the whole chicken he'd planned to have for dinner. He brought it to the sink, unwrapped it, and began rinsing it. He glanced over to see if Charley needed any help. She'd found his spice cabinet, and when she reached for the cinnamon bottle, he realized how he could sabotage her meal with Max. Right next to the cinnamon bottle was a similar one, only it held chili powder. The spices themselves looked quite a bit alike, and unless she purposely smelled the spice, an inexperienced cook wouldn't notice the difference. Damien opened his mouth to make sure she didn't grab the wrong bottle, but then snapped it close. The dinner would indeed be ruined if they used the chili powder instead of the cinnamon. Should he switch bottles when she wasn't looking?

He made the decision in a split second. "Sweetheart, why don't you go put one of my aprons on?"

"Great idea. Where do you keep them?"

"In the long closet right around the corner there. And grab me one while you're there."

As soon as she turned, he made the switch. Immediately, regret hit him like a punch in the stomach and he almost put the chili powder back. But then Charley returned, smiling sweetly, and he knew he'd do anything to keep Max from hurting her.

He proceeded to prepare the chicken, holding his breath when he sprinkled on the chili powder. Charley stood by the sink peeling the potatoes, so she didn't notice the pungent smell of the spice. She seemed a little preoccupied, humming a love song he'd heard recently on the radio. She was such a romantic.

After he set the chicken in the roaster and covered it with the lid, he picked up the pan. "I'm going to get this cooking in your oven. I'll be right back."

When he walked into her apartment, his heart sank. Candles and what looked to be her best plates and utensils were carefully arranged on a table for two in the middle of her living room. Music played in the background, and he realized why Charley had been humming that song.

Damien's hands tightened around the handles of the roaster. Would substituting chili powder for cinnamon be enough to ruin the evening? He doubted it, especially if Charley planned on dressing to kill.

He walked into the kitchen and turned on her oven, then placed the roasting pan inside. He released a heavy sigh. Tonight, he must tell her how he felt, and about Max. But should he confess his feelings this early in their friendship? It was a risk he would have to take, he decided.

He hurried to his townhouse to finish the dinner, telling Charley how to fix the potatoes while he cut up the broccoli.

Once she placed the potatoes in the casserole dish, he carried it to her house and placed it in the oven with the chicken. She followed behind with the pan of broccoli.

"Do you like how I set the table?" she asked excitedly.

"It's perfect."

She turned on the stove and put the lid on the broccoli. "Would you watch these steam while I get ready?"

He nodded.

She took a step away from him, then turned and launched herself into his arms, plopping a big kiss on his cheek. He closed his arms around her waist and held her against him, enjoying the moment.

"Oh, Damien, what would I do without you?" she said close to his ear.

Her warm breath teased his skin and made his heart leap. "I don't ever want to find out."

She pulled back and smiled. "You won't." She moved to kiss his cheek again, but he turned his head, letting her lips brush his mouth. He'd kissed her on the mouth once before, but this was different. This time she *knew* she was kissing him. No decongestants for an excuse this time!

She laughed and pulled away, seeming a bit breathless. But she turned and hurried down the hall to her bathroom before Damien could get a good look at her. Still, he could swear her cheeks had turned red.

He shook his head, then went back to the kitchen and readied the last-minute items she would need. From down the hall, her singing lifted through the apartment. She hit a few wrong notes and he smiled. He liked her because she wasn't perfect. She was Charley, and that was all that mattered.

The next half hour passed with irritating slowness, but finally the bathroom door opened. Damien had sat down on the couch, so he hurried into the kitchen to appear busy. When Charley's heels sounded on the kitchen floor, he turned to look at her. His breath caught in his throat.

"You're absolutely beautiful," he said in almost a whisper.

She blushed, fidgeting with the bodice of her white silk dress, then ran her hands down the straight skirt that ended just below her knees. She looked far different than the woman who'd gone to the Christmas party—very proper but sexy in her own way.

He shook his head. "Woman, you're going to make Max sit up and take notice."

Charley blushed. "Thanks. I'm glad you approve."

"Approve? I'm about ready to send you back in the bedroom to change into a nun's habit, young lady."

She laughed and nervously tucked a lock of hair behind her ear. He liked it when she kept her hair down, cascading over her shoulders.

"I look that good, huh?" she asked.

He stepped to her and grasped her hands in his. He gave her another once-over and whistled. "If I was Max, I'd never let you go."

"Really?"

"Really," he replied huskily.

She smiled and squeezed his hands. "Damien, I . . . I . . . really do love you, you know."

Keeping her hands in his, he lifted them to his mouth and kissed them. "Just as I love you."

The buzzer on the oven rang through the air and broke the magic spell between them. Damien grumbled under his breath and dropped Charley's hands, then turned to go into the kitchen.

Too bad he couldn't think of anything else to ruin her date with Max. He just hoped the chili-powdered chicken would do the trick. *All is fair in love and war.*

♡Chapter Eleven

Charley closed her eyes and breathed deeply, trying to calm her heart. Why did Damien have to look at her like that? His eyes were so dark, his expression so serious. When he'd told her he loved her, it was as if he'd meant it, not as a friend, but more.

The worst part was that she enjoyed it. No man had ever affected her the way Damien did. He surprised her at every turn. He seemed to genuinely care about her feelings, and although he would never admit it, he always thought of her first.

Did he act this way with other women he dated? Come to think of it, Charley hadn't seen a woman at his townhouse since the night he saved her from the thief. Had she judged Damien harshly? Perhaps she now saw his true character.

But Max was the one she was really interested in, she reminded herself as she turned to inspect the table settings.

Everything was perfect.

"Okay, I think everything's ready," Damien said suddenly. "But I think I'll let you do the serving."

"Thanks again for helping me."

He smiled and playfully cuffed her chin with his knuckles. "But remember, I don't wash dishes. That's your job."

Charley laughed. When he started to leave, she grabbed his arm. "Damien, before you go, um, about the other night, after the Christmas party . . . I need to know if you brought me home. I don't remember much, but I really don't think Max did."

"I brought you home."

She breathed a sigh of relief. "How did I act?"

"Like a woman who'd had one too many decongestants," he answered with a grin.

"Yes, I know that, but . . . but did I seem, uh, forward in any way?"

"Charley, where are you going with this?"

She huffed. "Just answer me, please. Did anything happen?"

"No. Nothing happened."

"Do you know if Max came to my apartment after you left?"

He shrugged. "It's possible. But why all the questions?"

"Because I don't want to say something stupid in front of Max tonight. When we talked yesterday at work, he acted as if he had been here."

Damien let out a brittle laugh. "Then maybe he had."

"But I want to know for sure. I don't want to say something and have him think I'm an idiot."

Damien shook his head. "He won't, and if he does—" he moved closer and cupped her face in his hands "—then he's not worth your time. You deserve someone who can love you for yourself. And you'd better make sure he does before you give your whole heart to him. I'd hate to see you miserable again."

She nodded. "I'll be careful."

He dropped a soft kiss on her mouth, his gentle lips brushing tingles across hers. It was all she could do to hold herself back from wrapping her arms around his neck. When he pulled away, she tried to hide her disappointment.

"I better go before he catches me here." Damien took a step back. "Don't do anything I wouldn't do." He winked, then turned and left.

As Charley marched into the bathroom to recheck her makeup, the memory of Damien's kiss returned, and she groaned aloud. She didn't want to fall in love with a man who would trample her heart when another Barbie wannabe came along. Plain and simple, Charley wanted a Mormon man who could take her to the temple.

She fluffed her hair the way Damien had done the night of the party. Suddenly, her doorbell buzzed and she jumped. She placed her hand over her chest to settle her erratic pulse.

Be yourself. Then again, Charley decided, that might be the worst thing she could do. She would just try not to mess up.

As she walked to the front door, she took a deep breath and said a quick prayer for courage. Then she pulled open the door and saw Max's handsome face. "Hello," she greeted. "Come in."

"Hi."

His gaze wandered over her, so she took a moment to inspect him closer. Instead of his usual business attire, he wore a long-sleeved blue-and-white-striped shirt with a collar. The first few buttons were unfastened, and his fingers were inside the front pockets of his jeans.

"You look really good," Max said.

Charley smiled. "I was just going to say the same thing to you." She took a step back and opened the door wider. "Come on in."

"Thought you'd never ask." He walked in and she closed the door behind him.

"Hmm. Smells good in here. What's for dinner? Something Mexican?"

"Not Mexican. Just a family recipe I threw together. I hope you like chicken."

"Love it."

"Go ahead and have a seat and I'll get the food." As Charley walked to the kitchen, she glanced over her shoulder and saw a smiling Max approach the table. So far, so good.

But why did he seem to be looking at her townhouse as if he'd never seen it before? If he *had* come to her place after the Christmas party, he wouldn't act like tonight was his first time here. And if neither he nor Damien had kissed her, had it all been a dream?

Charley shook off the thoughts and focused on dinner. Damien had taken the chicken and potatoes out of the oven and covered them to keep them warm.

She picked up the potatoes. From the other pan, something spicy assaulted her senses, making her stomach growl. *Chili powder?* Couldn't be! Her nerves were not only playing tricks on her body, but they were playing tricks on her senses as well.

Careful not to drop the dish, she carried the potatoes in the living room and set them on the table. Max leaned over and sniffed.

"Mmm. These smell heavenly. Don't tell me this is another family recipe. It smells like it came from a gourmet restaurant."

She chuckled. "Yes, this is just another family recipe."

Soon everything was arranged on the table, and the aroma from the chicken wafted through the air. Charley frowned. The chicken *did* smell like chili! Shouldn't it smell like cinnamon? She coughed to clear the lingering spice from her throat, willing away the threatening tears.

Max smiled. "This smells great."

Let's hope it tastes great, too, thought Charley.

"Are you sure this isn't a Mexican dish?" he asked.

"No. It's called cinnamon chicken."

She sat and adjusted the napkin on her lap then folded her arms. Max arched his brow at her and she smiled. "I think we should bless the food first, don't you?" she asked.

"Uh, sure." He looked at her oddly but folded his arms.

Charley bowed her head and said a quick prayer.

Back in high school, Max had been a faithful Church member. Yet from the way he acted, she guessed he hadn't prayed over his food in a very long time. Maybe he had fallen away from the Church, just like Damien. If so, Max wasn't the man she thought he was. She'd definitely have to ask more questions.

She reached over to spoon some potatoes on her plate. Max eagerly took a piece of chicken off the platter, licking his lips in anticipation. Suddenly, a feeling of dread hit her hard. Something would go wrong. She just knew it.

Max placed a large helping of potatoes on his plate before diving into his chicken. The red sauce dripped from his fingers when he picked up the leg and took a big bite. Charley held her breath.

When Max's eyes widened and he took a sharp breath, she knew something wasn't right. Quickly, he placed the chicken on the plate and picked up the pitcher of water, pouring the cool liquid into his glass. Tears pooled in his eyes before he could bring the drink to his mouth.

Charley licked some sauce off her finger. Her tongue burned like the Mexican border in the dead of summer. Instead of grabbing her water glass she quickly took a bite of potatoes. At least *they* tasted good.

Max wiped his mouth with his napkin and cleared his throat. "That's certainly a different-tasting chicken." He cleared his throat for the second time. "So, it's a family recipe, you say?"

Charley shrugged in humiliation. "Thought so, but now I'm wondering what I did wrong."

He took a large spoonful of potatoes, but said in between bites, "Didn't you say this was cinnamon chicken?"

"Yeah, I thought it was."

"Doesn't taste like cinnamon to me."

"Me either."

She tried to remember taking the spices from Damien's cupboard. Did she read the bottle or just look at the color? Inwardly, she groaned. She was willing to bet she'd picked up the chili powder instead.

"Oh, Max, I'm so sorry." She wiped the napkin across her mouth. "I think I put in chili powder instead of cinnamon."

He nodded and took another drink of his water. He didn't have to reply—the tears in his eyes made it all too clear. She'd failed again. At least Max was the only person to see her humiliation. Then again, he was the person in the world she wanted to impress the most.

She sighed and covered her face with her hands. Tears threatened to spill and a sob lodged in her throat. She just wanted the night to end. Then she could let him off the hook and tell him they'd just be friends. But she didn't want to be the office joke, either. If she gave up on Max, she'd never hear the end of it from Amanda—and whomever Amanda had told.

The screech of Max's chair sliding on the wooden floor made her jump. *He's leaving!*

But instead of walking out the door, he came around to her side and knelt beside her, taking her hands in his. "Charley, it's okay, really."

"How can you say that? I nearly gave your mouth third-degree burns."

He laughed. "No, you didn't. In fact, I like spicy foods. But I must confess, this is a little too hot even for me."

She laughed and then bit her bottom lip. "I wanted the meal to be perfect."

"It is. I really like the potatoes."

"What about the broccoli?"

"Well, I don't exactly like it, but I'll eat it."

She shook her head. "No, don't eat it. I've punished you enough for one night."

He kissed her cheek and then stood. "Then we'll have potatoes tonight."

"I have bread and butter."

"That's even better."

Although she knew Max was just being nice, Charley retrieved the bread and butter from the kitchen. He hated the meal, she could tell, but he still slopped down his food like a man in a hurry. She picked at her food like a bird; her nervous stomach wouldn't allow her to eat much.

Finally, he leaned back in his chair and linked his hands over his stomach. "Well, now that we're done, what else did you have planned?"

Maybe Charley was imagining things, but by the way he said it, it sounded like Max was hoping for more than dinner and dancing! He couldn't be *that* kind of man, could he? Didn't he know she didn't do things like that?

"Well, I hadn't really made any other plans."

"Why don't we watch the tube? TBS has a Stooges marathon tonight."

She raised her eyebrows. "Stooges?"

"Yeah, you know, *The Three Stooges*?"

"Oh, Larry, Moe, and Curly?"

"Exactly."

It sounded like a good idea, since number 6 from the article was funny movies, but she really didn't know that much about the Stooges. Before she could watch them with him, she'd better make sure she had watched a few of the movies herself. Then they'd have something to talk about.

Suddenly, she remembered number 5: *tall buildings.* Not too far from where she lived, there was a tall building with a restaurant on top. In fact, if she remembered correctly, the room moved around in a circle, giving a 360° view of the city.

She grinned. *Perfect.*

"I have a better idea," she said confidently.

"What's that?"

"How about dessert? I know this great restaurant up the street with a nice view of the city. Interested?"

"Yes," he replied with a wink.

Simultaneously, they pushed away from the table and stood. Charley grabbed her coat and purse as they headed to the front door, and Max opened the door and led her out.

The evening had started out bad, but Charley had definite hopes for a better ending.

♡Chapter Twelve

Tall Buildings

Damien walked to the front window and looked out at Charley's porch steps. He wondered how her night was going, and if the chicken had ruined her dinner with Max. He glanced down at his wristwatch. It had only been a half hour since the date started, so Max was probably still there.

With a huff, Damien moved away from the window. Why was he sulking like this? He'd never acted this way over a woman. Of course, he'd never met a woman like Charlene Randall. Unlike most women he knew, she wasn't trying to get a man for his money but instead wanted to find one to fill the void in her life.

The void in his life needed to be filled, too. A different woman every other day had been getting old for a while now. He wanted a relationship with one woman. Forever.

As he turned and reached for his black leather jacket behind the door, Damien wondered if he was in love with Charley. He wanted to date her and had wanted that for a while now, but sometimes he wondered if it was because she wasn't interested in him—because she was a challenge. Yet spending so much time with her over the last several days had made him happy.

With a heavy sigh, Damien admitted the truth to himself. He did love her. And he wanted to be the kind of man she wanted, a man who would take her to the temple. The problem was, she still wanted Max.

After slipping on his jacket, Damien went outside. The cool wind blew against his face and he bundled the collar around his neck, trying to block out the chill. Tonight was certainly not the kind of weather for walking, but he hoped it would cool his aggravation. He walked down the street until a large building loomed before him. The Franklin Hotel was famous for the revolving restaurant on its top floor. Once inside the five-star hotel, Damien unzipped his jacket and waited in front of the elevators. When Damien entered the restaurant lobby, the aroma of steak made his stomach growl. He scanned the tables as he waited for the hostess to seat him and was surprised to see a familiar white dress and the woman who had filled his dreams lately.

Charley leaned forward with her arms resting on the table, laughing at something Max had said. Damien fisted his hands and shoved them into the pockets of his jacket.

Looks like she won her man.

But Damien couldn't let Max use her. All during college, Max was the man who jumped from one woman to another. Damien's so-called friend even went after women who were taken. And, like an idiot, Damien didn't notice when the woman who was supposed to have loved him started spending more time with Max.

He gritted his teeth. He wouldn't let Charley go through that. She deserved better. For the last six months, he'd watched as men traipsed in and out of her life, and he knew she wanted someone to settle down with. Max wasn't the settling-down type and never would be.

Damien pivoted on his heels to head back to the elevator but ran into a woman. He grasped her thin shoulders to keep her from teetering, and when the dark-haired woman looked up at him, he quickly dropped his hands to his sides.

"Damieno?" Liza exclaimed. "Fancy bumping into you here."

"Yes, what a surprise. Are you here alone?" He couldn't believe she wasn't hanging on some rich man's arm.

"Yes and no. I'm actually waiting for my friends. They were going to meet me, but I've been waiting ten minutes and they haven't arrived." She looked over his shoulder, then back into his eyes. "Where's your date?"

"I—I didn't come with a date."

"Really? Why not?"

It was none of her business what was happening in his life. "I guess you can say I was stood up too. So if you'll excuse me, I'll be leaving."

"Damieno, wait—" Liza grabbed his elbow before he could walk past her. "Since we've both been stood up, let's eat together."

He glanced at Charley's table; thankfully, she wasn't looking his way. Although dining with Liza was the last thing in the world he wanted to do, he welcomed the excuse to stay to keep an eye on Charley.

He looked back at Liza and nodded. "Fine, but I'm here only to eat. Don't read any more into this."

She smiled and hooked her arm around his. "Oh, Damieno, Why would I read more into it? We're just old friends."

The hostess escorted them to a table. When they headed in Charley's direction, Damien grimaced, hoping she wouldn't see him. Luckily, her back was to him when they passed her table.

When they reached their table, just a few tables away from Charley's, Damien slid into a chair. Lifting the menu to cover his face, he ignored the fact that Liza waited by her chair to be seated.

With a huff, she finally pulled out her chair and sat, bumping the table in the process. Damien peeked over the top of the menu, first at Liza's scowl, then beyond her to Charley's table. The object of his dreams still stared into Max's eyes. Damien breathed a sigh of relief that she hadn't seen him.

"Damieno," Liza whispered harshly. "What's wrong with you?"

He looked around the edge of the menu and smiled at her. "Nothing."

She shook her head. "Liar. You're trying to hide."

"Nah, I'm just reading the menu."

To prove it, he relaxed in his chair, keeping the menu high, but not completely covering his face. He couldn't read a thing and decided he needed to make an appointment with the optometrist. Then he realized the problem and slowly turned the menu right side up.

"Hmm . . . everything looks good. What are you going to have?" He peeked at Liza.

When she opened her menu and gazed down at it, Damien took the opportunity to spy on Charley and Max. He had a side view of both of their faces, and Charley looked absolutely stunning as she smiled up at Max. Then she laughed at something Max said, and the cheerful ring to her voice floated across the room. Damien sighed, wishing he was her date instead of Max.

"Damieno? Are you listening to me?"

He snapped out of his daydream. "Yes."

"Then what did I say?"

139

He grinned. "You said you're not hungry and you want to go home."

She rolled her eyes. "No, I didn't, and you know it. I said I'm ordering the vegetarian plate."

"Oh, in that case, I'll order steak and potatoes."

Tilting her head, she crossed her arms over her chest. "Why are you annoying me?"

He shrugged. "Old habit?"

"When we were together, you were never this mean." She reached across the table and pulled the menu out of his hands.

Damien ducked lower, trying to keep Liza between himself and Charley, so Charley wouldn't see him.

Liza squeezed his hand. "Back then, you were so charming and loving."

He looked at his ex. "Back then I was stupid enough to be taken in by your beauty. Back then I didn't know what I wanted in my life. Now I do." He withdrew his hand from her grasp and stared out the window. The gathering clouds made the sky darker, which in turn made the lighted city brighter. Slowly, the neighboring buildings crept by as the restaurant rotated, and, once again, Damien wished he could share this with Charley.

Across from him, Liza cleared her throat, so he looked at her. *Poor woman can't stand that I'm not hanging on her every word.*

"Damieno, have you thought anymore about my offer?"

"What offer?"

"You know what offer I'm referring to."

He shook his head. "There is no offer, Liza. I don't make deals with the devil."

Her lips pursed, her fingers tightening around the cloth napkin on the table. "Would you for once in your life think logically?"

"I've been thinking logically since I caught you in Max's

arms." He narrowed his gaze on her. "In fact, I've never thought more clearer than I do now."

"So you're going to ignore everything I'm offering you?"

"It appears that way, doesn't it?"

"I could make you a wealthy man."

He laughed sarcastically. "Liza, I'm wealthy enough, thank you very much. So tell me, was I right the other day when I guessed your attempts to open your own manufacturing plant in Colorado failed?"

Her brow furrowed. "How did you know about Colorado?"

"Don't you remember that I always kept track of my competitors?" Damien shook his head. "If you can't keep an eye on your competitors, you may as well give up your business altogether."

With a huff, Liza folded her arms and leaned back in her chair. The waiter came to take their orders. Damien ordered the ten-ounce steak smothered in sautéed mushrooms.

When the waiter left, Damien glanced back at Charley's table. She had her head turned to look out the window, as did Max. Damien noticed Max looked a bit pale, and he wondered if Mr. Sports was ill—or afraid of heights.

Damien grinned wider. Maybe Max felt his head spinning at this very moment! Damien could only hope.

"Whom are you looking at? You have such an evil grin on your face." Liza looked over her shoulder to search the room.

"No one."

He didn't want Liza to know what he couldn't keep his eyes off, but he didn't look away quick enough. Besides, it was comical to watch Max's face grow whiter as the room continued to move. Damien placed a hand over his mouth to keep from laughing.

"Oh, my." Liza gasped. "Isn't that Maxwell Harrington?"

"In the flesh."

"Why are you watching him?"

He shrugged. "No reason, really. He's just having dinner with my next-door neighbor, Charlene Randall."

Suddenly, as Damien watched, Charley reached across the table to touch Max's arm, but Max quickly withdrew and knocked over his drink.

Charley jumped up and dabbed the wet tablecloth with her napkin. Two waiters rushed to her table.

Max stood and took a step back. He swayed.

Damien leaned his elbows on the table, watching, waiting. *He's going down for the count.*

Max's knees buckled and he dropped. Gasps echoed around the room.

Charley hurried to Max's side and patted his cheeks. One of the waiters took a glass of water and splashed some on Max's face. Damien heard a sick groan from Max. *Poor guy.*

"Do you think we should go over?" Liza asked.

Damien shook his head, keeping his eyes on Charley. "It looks as if Charley and the waiter have it handled."

Charley's beautiful face was pulled tight in worry. Damien would be there for her later, and maybe he would finally confess his true feelings.

Charley wearily pulled herself into her townhouse and closed the door. She dropped her purse and keys on the entryway table, then dragged herself to the couch and collapsed.

What a night!

She buried her head in a throw pillow. *Way to get your date sick, Charley.* How could she know Max was afraid of heights? Why didn't he just say something? It wouldn't have hurt her feelings to go to another restaurant.

She'd messed up number 5 from the internet list. Did she dare attempt number 6?

Groaning, she rolled over on the couch and looked at the television. Max had mentioned a *Three Stooges* marathon on TBS. She sat up and tucked her legs under her, then grabbed the remote, switched on the television, and turned it to the correct station.

As Larry, Moe, and Curly slapped and kicked each other, Charley studied them closely. Max thought this was funny? Well, it was funny if pie-in-the-face humor was your kind of thing, but it really wasn't something she wanted to sit through for more than a few minutes.

The light tapping on her door jerked her attention away from the television. She glanced at the clock on the wall. It was 1:00 a.m.

"Charley?"

Leave it to Damien to check up on her. She stood and walked to the door to let him in.

When he entered, he scanned the living room. "Am I interrupting anything?"

"No," Charley answered as she returned to the couch.

He shut the door and sauntered over to join her, a shirt draped over his arm.

"What's that for?" she asked.

"I just wondered if you could sew a button on for me. I'm no good at that kind of thing."

"Sure, I'd love to."

"So why am I not interrupting anything?" Damien took her hand and squeezed it.

"Because, as always, I messed things up." Her voice cracked and she held back a sob.

He laid the shirt on the edge of the couch, then sat closer to Charley. "Come here and tell me about it."

Damien's invitation was too good to pass up. She cuddled next him, pressing her face against his chest. He gently stroked her hair, and she relaxed, though she still felt mortified about Max.

"Now tell me what happened," Damien said in a soft voice.

Charley hiccupped a laugh. "I don't know if you realized it while making the chicken tonight, but I mistakenly gave you the chili powder instead of the cinnamon."

His body froze. "You did?"

"Yes, but Max only took a couple of bites before realizing it was too spicy for him."

"Oh, honey, I'm sorry." His arm tightened around her shoulders and his warm breath brushed the top of her head.

"But the rest of the meal turned out fine. Well, except he doesn't like broccoli."

Damien tried not to smile. "Then what happened?"

"I remembered another way to win a man's heart—from the Internet article, of course—was to take him to a tall building. The article mentioned how guys like tall things. Anyway, I remembered the Franklin Hotel had a revolving restaurant on the top floor, so we went there."

"Sounds romantic."

"Yeah, well, I thought so too, but it wasn't."

"Why not?"

"Believe it or not, Max is afraid of heights, and sitting right by the window made him sick." Charley pulled back and looked up at Damien. "He even passed out."

She saw Damien's lip twitch. "Don't you dare laugh."

"I'm trying not to."

When she felt a smile coming on too, she quickly lowered her cheek back to his chest before he could see. "It's not funny."

"No, it's not. I'm sure he was very humiliated."

"He was, and so was I."

For a few minutes, the only sound was the *Three Stooges* on the TV.

"I didn't know you were into the Stooges," Damien said.

"I'm not, but I'm trying to be."

"Why?"

"Because Max is." She lifted her head and looked at Damien again. "The sixth way to win a man is to share his favorite movies.

He nodded toward the television. "And do you share his interest?"

She glanced over her shoulder at the program. "I really haven't gotten into it yet. I don't understand why they have to hit each other all the time, and why he—" she pointed to the dark-haired man with the funny haircut "—has to act so tough. He's more stupid than tough."

Damien laughed. "Exactly. In fact, if you'll look at all those older comedians, you'll see they're the same way. Look at Laurel and Hardy, Abbott and Costello, even Jerry and Dean."

"True." Charley noticed the softness in his brown eyes. "Who's your favorite comedian?"

"I have a few. I like Abbott and Costello, and my favorite is Wayne Brady."

She gasped and sat up straight. "No kidding. Mine, too."

His smile grew. "No kidding."

"Isn't that funny?"

"Yes, very."

She stared into his eyes. Her heartbeat quickened and her mouth turned dry. His gaze dropped to her lips, and she wanted to lean forward and kiss him. She shook away the thought. She couldn't fall for him!

145

"Charley?"

"Yes?"

"What happened after the date tonight? Did Max kiss you goodnight?" Damien's voice was tight.

She frowned. "No. He didn't feel very well, so I didn't push the issue."

"Do you still think he's the one?"

"I don't know. I'm starting to have doubts."

"Why?" Damien's hand moved over her hair in soft strokes.

"Because I can't seem to be myself around him." She drew tiny circles on his chest with her finger. "I wish I could act normal, but I'm nervous all the time, and you know what happens when I get nervous."

"Yes, I know." Damien chuckled.

"And he's just not the person I thought I knew."

"What do you mean?"

"Well, when I had a crush on Max in high school, he was also in my stake, and I saw him at all the stake youth activities. I know he went to church. In school, he went to seminary classes." She shrugged. "Now, little things he does makes me wonder if he's not an active member of the Church—if he doesn't believe anymore."

"What if he doesn't?" Damien asked softly.

Charley lifted her gaze and met his eyes. "That would make a big difference, Damien. I want to date a man who is committed to the Church, as I try to be. I want to be sealed in the temple. And I know it sounds crazy, but I would rather die single than marry outside of my religion."

"Have you asked him about it?"

"Not yet."

"Well, maybe you should."

She studied Damien's face, wondering if she dared ask *him*

the same question. Finally, she blurted out, "Damien, what about you?"

"What? You want me to ask Max if he's still going to church?"

She slapped his arm playfully. "No, silly! I mean, do you ever think about getting married and having a family? And have you ever thought of going back to church?"

Damien took her hand and held it, tenderly caressing her knuckles. "You're not going to believe this, but yes, I've thought about getting married and raising a family." He smiled. "And lately, well, I've even considered going back to church."

Her heart leapt. "You have? Why?"

He leaned his head back against the couch and stared up at the ceiling. "I'm tired of the way I've been living my life. I'm tired of not having a serious relationship." He turned his head to look at her. "It got boring after a while, you know—going out with a different woman almost every night. Nothing in my life has made sense, and I feel like I've been in a rut." He chuckled and shook his head. "Believe it or not, I picked up the Book of Mormon the other day and started reading. And I prayed."

Charley thought her heart would burst, but she tried not to overreact. "Damien, that's great. Do you want to start coming to church with me?"

He grinned. "Sure, if you don't mind."

"I don't mind at all. I think it would be great. In fact, I'll invite Max."

His grin quickly disappeared, and she realized too late that she'd said the wrong thing.

"Charley, I'm not ready to talk to Max on a personal level, but I think it's a good idea if you ask him to go to church with you."

She nodded. "I will. I'm not giving up on him until he gives me some kind of signal that he's not interested in me."

Damien sat up and cupped her chin in his hand. "Who wouldn't be interested in Charlene Randall? You're every man's dream."

She snorted. "Every man's nightmare, you mean."

"Quit being hard on yourself."

"Can't help it. I'm an accident on parade."

"No, you're not."

She pulled away and sat up straight. "I suppose I should tell you about my ex, James."

"What happened?"

"I started a fire in his apartment. Sure, it was only a grease fire, but still—"

Damien frowned. "Then I'm certain the fire was put out quickly."

"True, but I still caused it. I could have burned down his whole apartment building." Damien opened his mouth to continue, but she held up a hand to stop him. "And that's not all. Guess what happened with Timothy?"

"What?"

"He broke his leg sliding down my back steps. They were covered with ice."

"You can't blame yourself for that," Damien said. "He should have seen the ice and been careful."

She shook her head. "He would have walked down the stairs just fine if I hadn't tripped on the doormat and plowed into him." She folded her arms across her chest. "Shall I go on?"

"No, Charley. Stop it right now. All of those things were accidents."

"Oh, come on, Damien—"

"Charlene." He cupped his hand over her mouth. "If I hear one more word about this, I'm taking you over my knee."

A giggle erupted from her throat. She pulled back and his hand dropped. "And do what, may I ask?"

He grinned. "Keep belittling yourself and you'll find out."

She pouted teasingly and poked him in the ribs. "Oh, you're so mean."

He put his arms around her. "Charley, the plain and simple truth is those other guys weren't right for you. You'll find the man of your dreams, and you'll know it because you can be yourself around him. If a man can't love you for the Charley I know, he's not worth it."

Her chest tightened. *If Damien is starting to read the scriptures and pray again,* Charley thought, *I can consider dating him!* Then she shook her head. As much as she would like Damien to change, she couldn't give on Max yet. She had to give it one more shot to find out if they could hit it off.

♡ Chapter Thirteen

Funny Movies

Strikeout number 6. Charley had expected to at least make it all the way through an inning, but it didn't look good.

She shoved the car into PARK and killed the engine, then glanced up and down the dark street. She heaved a sigh and slumped her head forward to knock it against the steering wheel.

What was wrong with her? Why couldn't she make anything go right? She'd had it all planned out this morning. She'd invite Max to lunch, and during their meal she'd bring up the Stooges. Well, that part had gone well. Max had picked the restaurant, an out-of-the-way Greek place not too far from work. It was semi-crowded, but she had expected that.

She'd been extremely nervous. She almost had to sit on her hands because they shook so hard. But once she and Max started discussing the Stooges, she breathed easier. In fact, she thought it was brilliant when he asked her a question and she threw out a Curly phrase: "Why soitenly! N'yuck, n'yuck, n'yuck."

Max had laughed over that, so she continued with one of Moe's: "Why, you lamebrain, I'll fracture ya." Moe always threatened to do bodily harm.

Max had thrown back his head and laughed heartily. She went on with the name-calling: mashed potato muscles, two-ounce brain, little man, and cabbage head. Since Max seemed to enjoy her play acting, she decided to move in for the kill. "Prepare for 81-c!" She held out a hand, two fingers extended, and aimed for his eyes.

Thinking back, Charley growled in embarrassment and pounded her head on the steering wheel. Was it her fault Max forgot to block her fingers? After all, he was a Stooges fan. He should have known.

She lifted her head and rubbed the sore spot just below her hairline. Perhaps she'd hit her head a little too hard that time. Yet she deserved it. Poor Max couldn't open his eyes for at least ten minutes after she'd gouged them.

Tears threatened, and it wasn't because of the pain in her head. Plain and simple, she was a loser. She couldn't do anything right when it came to men.

Reluctantly, she opened the door and climbed out of her car. When she slammed the door, the echo rang through the deserted street.

A tear slipped free and was soon joined by several dozen others. Charley clutched her purse to her chest, trying to hold back a sob. Before she reached her door, Damien's door opened and he stepped out on the porch.

"Charley? What's wrong?"

The concern in his voice increased the ache in her heart, and her tears fell freely once again. He held his arms open and she rushed to him, pressing her face against his black leather jacket. His embrace tightened around her.

"Mi amore, what's wrong?" he repeated tenderly.

She couldn't say a word so he lifted her in his arms and stepped back into his townhouse. He took her to his couch and sat.

The gentle stroke of his hand in her hair soothed her cries. She remained in his lap, and scolded herself for enjoying every second of it.

But she loved him.

How did this happen? I don't want to love him!

She took a deep breath, then lifted her head and gazed into Damien's eyes. Her heart clenched. She wanted him in her life. She wanted him to love her, to devote himself to her and only her. Would he ever do that? Would he love her enough to take her to the temple and be sealed to her for time and all eternity? And then would he live the gospel and serve the Lord the rest of their lives?

He wiped his thumb over her cheek, brushing away more tears. "Please tell me what's wrong."

"I'm up to strike 6. Good thing I'm not playing baseball, huh?"

"What happened?"

Her forced laugh sounded pathetic. "You wouldn't think I could mess this one up, but I did."

"Did you talk to him about the Stooges?"

"Yes."

"He didn't like it?"

"Oh, he liked it, all right. He thought my version of Curly's 'n'yuck, n'yuck, n'yuck' was amusing."

"Then what went wrong?" Damien asked.

"I thought, being a Stooge fan and all, that he'd be prepared when I did the fingers-in-the-eyes trick." She shook her head. "He wasn't. His eyes watered for nearly a half hour, and even when he left work, they were still red. If he goes blind, it'll be my fault."

Damien's lips twitched, and even through her misery, a smile tugged at Charley's lips.

"Oh, Damien, why didn't Max block my poke?" She rubbed her forehead and sighed.

"I don't know, mi amore." He pushed a lock of hair behind her ear. "Perhaps at this very moment he's kicking himself for not doing it."

"Oh, I'm sure he's doing a lot more than kicking himself. He's probably at the eye doctor discussing treatment options."

Damien shook his head. "Charley, I love your sense of humor."

Her heartbeat quickened. Instinctively, she reached out to touch Damien's square, clean-shaven jaw, cupping the side of his face with her hand. His cheek was smooth against her palm, and she imagined how it would feel against her cheek. Why did the picture in her mind seem so real?

Was he in her townhouse the night of the Christmas party? Had it been his hands cupping her face, his lips kissing her? *Yes.* She knew it now, and the knowledge left her heart pounding almost out of control.

She stared at his lips, remembering the way they had touched hers. It hadn't been a dream! They had shared some very sweet, gentle kisses.

Now, his expression softened and his lips parted. Charley leaned forward slowly, waiting for him to stop her, but he didn't. She threaded her fingers through his hair, pulled his face to hers, and kissed him tenderly. This was exactly what her dream had been like, only this time her heart soared even higher.

"Oh, Charley," Damien mumbled between kisses, "I've dreamed of doing this for so long."

"Damien," she whispered his name just to hear it on her lips. She touched the side of his face and he nuzzled against her palm, kissing her skin.

She urged his face back to hers, but just before they could kiss again, his cell phone chirped, making her jump. She held his stare during the second ring, but by the third, a scowl had replaced his smile.

He lifted himself off the couch, grabbed the cell clipped to his waist, and quickly read the caller ID. Grumbling, he answered on the fourth ring. "This better be a life-threatening emergency."

Within seconds, his expression changed. Now he looked worried. "Fine. I'll be there shortly."

He sighed and closed the phone. When he met Charley's stare, he gave her a half smile. "I hate to bring this to an end, but that was work."

"Are you in trouble or something?" she asked.

"No, mi amore." He leaned down and brushed his lips across hers. "I'd like to finish our little discussion later, if that's all right."

She nodded. "How long before you're done at work?"

"It'll be around midnight. Is that too late?"

"No."

He touched his finger to her lips, stroking them softly. "Please stay here until I return. We have a lot to discuss." He winked and then left his townhouse.

A giddy laugh sprang from her throat and she hugged the throw pillow to her chest. The evening looked brighter already.

Damien stormed into his office, slamming the door behind him. That conniving woman was at it again. If Liza's company was in the hole, how did she find all this money to start buying out his stocks? He would not have it! Liza Scapolli needed to be stopped.

Damien's mother had called to tell him Liza was buying up stock in his company. Sure, his mother's call had come at an inopportune moment, but she couldn't help that.

Thinking of Charley, he smiled. He didn't like that she might be on the rebound from Max. If they continued on the path they were on before he left his townhouse, wouldn't he just be taking advantage of her again? He would and he knew it. Just like that night after the party.

The tender emotion in Charley's eyes flitted through Damien's mind and he groaned. How was he supposed to resist her? Besides, wasn't this what he wanted?

Her kisses melted his heart, and he'd never felt that before. Sure, he'd been attracted to other women, but with Charley it was different. She was everything he'd dreamed about and more. Tonight he'd come clean and tell her the truth—that he'd been in love with her for quite a while. He would even tell her he owned GIO Products, instead of letting her think he just worked for the company.

Two swift knocks sounded on the door, interrupting his reverie. His mother rushed into his office, wringing her hands. "Damieno, what are we to do?"

"Mother, I can't control the shareholders of the company. If they choose to sell their stock to Liza, there's nothing I can do."

"Stop her somehow. Make a deal with her. I don't care what, but do something."

He ran his fingers through his hair, then sank farther into his brown leather chair. He leaned forward, linking his fingers and resting them on the desk, trying hard to concentrate, trying not to think about Charley.

"What's so wrong with bringing her on as a partner?" his mother was saying. "We could write the contract up so she'd only get forty-eight percent of the stock."

Damien scowled. "No. I won't have her back in my life, trying to steal ideas from me again."

"It might not be that way now."

He arched an eyebrow and tilted his head. "What way do you think it will be, then? That woman is Satan's own sister!"

"Damieno, watch your mouth in front of your mother."

"Please forgive me, Mother, but when speaking about that woman, my tongue gets carried away. An old habit, I suppose."

"I have an idea." Bella walked around to his side of the desk and reached over to click on his computer. "Look up the rest of the shareholders she hasn't swayed yet, and call an emergency meeting. Maybe then we'll figure out what can be done to stop her."

He nodded and brought up the spreadsheet that contained their addresses and phone numbers. "Brilliant idea."

She nudged him with her elbow. "Yeah, I'm surprised you didn't think of it first."

"I've had other things on my mind." He couldn't help but smile.

His mother leaned forward and took his chin, turning his head to look at her. Finally, a smile stretched across her mouth. "You're in love, aren't you?"

Damien pulled away to look back at the computer screen. "Yes, Mother. I can't lie to you."

"Who is she?"

"She's my next-door neighbor."

His mother gave a hearty laugh. "So Michelle was right. When do I get to meet this young woman?"

He glanced over his shoulder at his mother. "Should we wait until we get this mess cleaned up with Liza first?"

"Yes, but you better hurry. With news like this, I can't wait much longer."

♡Chapter Fourteen

Mend His Clothes/Surprise Intimacy

How did Charley get so lucky? The man she'd grown close to as a best friend was now within her grasp. She thought about how she loathed him upon meeting him, because he'd been a womanizer, but somehow his attitude about life had changed. He'd changed.

Or had she been the one to transform?

And what about Max—why was it so easy to dismiss him from her mind? Had she subconsciously known all this time that he wasn't the right guy for her? Had he simply been a challenge, an experiment? She'd never once felt comfortable around him, and all she ever seemed to do was stumble over her words and cause him bodily harm. Damien had been right. The perfect man would be the one she could be herself with.

Damien was so attentive, so loving, caring, and thoughtful. He listened to her, shared in her sorrow, and made her laugh when she needed it. Best of all, he made her feel good about herself.

And what about the point she was trying to prove to Amanda, to her coworkers? She'd failed to find any success with the Internet article on how to win a man. Almost everything she tried on Max had been a disaster. In the meantime, Damien had melted and won her heart.

She smiled. What her coworkers said didn't matter. Damien was the only person who mattered.

After Damien left, Charley tried watching television, but she was so excited she couldn't concentrate. Since she wanted to get to know him better, she decided to look through the books stacked on the small bookshelf in the corner of the room. Near the top of one pile of books, one caught her attention. The Book of Mormon.

Damien had mentioned he'd started reading the Book of Mormon again, and that he wanted to go back to church. That made Charley happy.

She took the Book of Mormon to the sofa and sat, but as she started to read, the words ran together. Even though she loved the scriptures, she just couldn't concentrate right now.

What else could she do? She really wasn't hungry. There wasn't anything else to do but pace the floor, wringing her hands in nervous anticipation.

She'd promised to stay at Damien's house, but it drove her crazy not to be doing anything. At least if she was home, she could soak in a hot, bubble-filled tub. She searched for an extra set of house keys, and when she found them, she left the townhouse, locking the door behind her.

When she entered her place, the first thing she saw was Damien's shirt lying across the back of her couch. He'd wanted her to sew on a button. With a smile, she rushed around the house until she located her sewing kit, then sat cross-legged on her bed and went to work.

Once she was done, she studied her handiwork, proud of herself. Damien would approve.

Oh, Damien. She sighed and fell back on the bed, her thoughts turning to their first kiss—the kiss she almost didn't remember. She'd have to ask him why he didn't say anything. Suddenly, dread washed over her and she bolted into a sitting position. *I called out Max's name.*

No wonder Damien didn't say anything about it! She didn't blame him one bit for leading her to believe she'd kissed Max. Served her right for being such a fool. Now she had to make it up to him somehow.

Damien must have forgiven her, Charley decided; otherwise he wouldn't have kissed her with so much feeling tonight. She smiled and scooted off the bed. As she looked at his shirt, she wondered what it would look like on her. With a giggle, she threw off her own shirt and slipped into his, buttoning up the front. It could have been a nightshirt for her, since the bottom reached halfway to her knees. Wearing his shirt made her feel almost as if he had his arms wrapped around her right now.

Number 8—surprise intimacy. Charley smiled. Did she dare let Damien see her wearing his shirt? It would be a bold move that would make it clear she wanted to be an intimate part of his life. But she only wanted to be with him as his wife and as the future mother of his children, and she didn't know how he'd feel about those conditions.

She walked the floor in her townhouse, but by 1:00 a.m. she decided Damien wasn't coming. Maybe he had changed his mind already. Or maybe he really didn't have a work emergency but had gone to see another woman.

Shaking her head, Charley pushed away the doubts. He wouldn't do that to her, not after the friendship and trust they had built. Maybe the reason he hadn't returned was because something terrible had happened. No, she wouldn't think about that, either. She'd go to bed and hopefully see Damien in the morning.

She turned off the stereo, then flipped off the living room lights except one small lamp near the couch. A sudden knock at the front door sent her heart into her throat. "Yes?" she called hesitantly.

"Charley, it's me."

She recognized Damien's voice and quickly unlocked and opened the door. The porch light was dim, and shadows darkened his face. He'd flung his black leather jacket over his shoulder and held it with one finger.

His gaze moved over her slowly, and a lazy grin touched his mouth. "That shirt looks better on you than it does on me." He gave her a wink. "Have I interrupted something?"

She laughed. "Yes. Can't you tell I'm just about ready to curl up in bed with a good book?"

He stepped closer until he was a breath away. She looked into his warm brown eyes.

He cupped her chin, staring at her lips. "Lucky book."

"I thought I'd been stood up. When a man tells a woman a time, he'd better stick to it."

"The meeting ran later than I'd thought." His thumb stroked her bottom lip. "Will you forgive me?"

"Yes, as long as you do something for me."

"What's that?" His tender voice sent chills down her spine.

"Come inside. You're freezing me to death with the door open." She stepped back for him to enter then shut the door behind him.

He threw his jacket over the small table and took her in his arms. "Are you still cold?" he asked.

"I'm getting warm now, thank you."

He took her hand in his and led her to the couch. When he

sat, he pulled her down beside him, wrapping an arm around her shoulders as he brought her close.

She tilted her head to look at him, but he lowered his mouth to hers. Closing her eyes, she kissed him, her heart bursting with joy. She realized she'd never truly been in love until now, and she wanted to tell Damien so badly her chest ached.

When Damien finally pulled away, he smiled. "I think we need to talk."

"We do."

"There is something I need to tell you." He gave her a peck on the lips.

"And I, you."

She gazed into his dark eyes. He cupped her chin and tilted it up.

"What did you want to tell me, mi amore?"

"I remember what happened the night of the Christmas party."

His eyes widened. "You do?"

"Yes. As much as you tried to make me think otherwise, I know it was you. You were the one who kissed me, not Max."

Damien smiled but didn't speak.

She continued. "I want to apologize for saying Max's name in the middle of our kiss. I don't know why I said it, because you were the one on my mind. You were the one in my dreams and making me giddy with excitement. I can't believe I couldn't see what was in front of me the whole time."

His eyes widened even more. "Really?"

"Really. I'd been thinking of you for a few days, and I was pretty confused, because I thought I liked Max. But I'd actually been thinking of kissing you, not him."

"Promise?"

"Yes."

"Why didn't you tell me sooner?"

"Because once we became good friends," she said with a shrug, "I figured you weren't interested in me any other way."

"And because you thought I couldn't commit to one woman?"

"Yes, I'll admit I thought you were a player."

"I wasn't looking for a relationship, but I guess being with all those women—never committing to anyone—was my way of protecting myself from money-hungry women like my ex."

"What happened? What did she do to make you that way?"

He held Charley's hand in his, stroking her fingers. "Liza Scapolli isn't a very nice woman. Of course, I didn't know that at the time. She was only after me for one thing—to collect information about GIO Products to take back to her boyfriend, who was creating his own company, Herbal Sensations."

"How awful."

"That wasn't the worst of it. I caught her in an intimate embrace with my so-called best friend."

She sucked in a quick breath and frowned. "Really?"

"Yes."

"Oh, Damien! That's just terrible."

He nodded. "The man I caught her with was Max."

Charley felt like a building had fallen on top of her. "Max?"

"Yes."

So that was why Damien didn't like Max! "Why didn't you tell me sooner?" Charley asked, realizing how much Damien must care for her, to help her win a man who had betrayed him in the worst possible way.

Damien's fingers threaded through her hair and he pulled her face closer to his. "I didn't want you to think the only reason I disapproved of Max was because of my past dealings with him. If you remember right, you were not very fond of me at that time."

She grimaced. "True."

"Now let me ask you, Charley. What about Max? Are you over him?"

She lowered her gaze to his neck, then touched the top button on his shirt. "To be honest with you, I don't think I was ever really into winning his heart. At the time, I was angry with Amanda for suggesting I couldn't keep a man longer than three months. Max was a challenge. Plus I wanted to prove to myself I could keep a man."

"What about me?" Damien asked.

She met his stare.

"What am I to you? A challenge? A friend?"

"A friend, yes, but so much more than that," Charley responded. "You're not a challenge, yet I wouldn't mind seeing how far we could take our relationship."

"What do you want now?"

She smiled. "I don't want to be just your friend anymore." She slid her hands around and grasped the back of his head to gently pull him closer. "I want to be with you for—for a very long time. I just pray it's something you might want as well. If not, let me know now—"

Damien stopped her words with another kiss, so she leaned into him and wrapped her arms around her neck. His kiss sent her floating to the clouds and back.

Soon, he pulled away with a serious look on his face. "I do want what you want, Charley. Being with you has made me remember what it was like to trust in the Lord, in His guidance. Charley, I really want to go back to church. Will you help me?"

She squealed and threw her arms around him and kissed him hard. "That's what I wanted to hear. Of course I'll help you."

He caressed her cheek. "You have made me want to change,

Charley. I like the way I feel when I'm with you, and I don't ever want that to go away."

"That will never happen. I promise."

Charley arrived at work on cloud nine, and she had to force herself not to skip to her office. A few coworkers raised their eyebrows at her, but she just giggled and waved. Yes, she had a man in her life, and she planned on keeping this one.

She realized now why she hadn't kept the others. She hadn't felt comfortable being herself—her clumsy, silly self. But with Damien, she had. He accepted her for who she was. That's one of the reasons she loved him so much.

The first few hours of the day, she couldn't stop smiling and could hardly wait to see Damien again. She prayed he loved her as much as she did him. He wanted to attend church with her, and that was the best surprise of all.

The morning's breaking news stories kept the office jumping. Charley had been on the phone contacting witnesses and searching for more leads about a carjacking.

During lunch she found a moment to relax, so she called Damien on his cell. She got his voicemail, so she looked up the number for GIO Products and dialed it. When she asked for Damien, a secretary informed her he was in a meeting.

She laid her head back against the couch in the break room and clicked off her phone. He'd never really told her what he did at GIO, but he must be a supervisor of some sort. It could explain how he had enough money to redecorate his townhouse.

Charley rolled her neck to relax the tight muscles. Just then, the break room door squeaked open. Max entered and headed for the soda machine, obviously not noticing Charley curled up on the couch. He looked nice as always, but she was relieved that her heart didn't leap at the sight of him. Now she could treat him like she treated her other coworkers.

After the soda can rolled from the machine into his hand, Max straightened and turned. At least both of his eyes were in place, and he didn't look like he'd gone blind from her poking him the day before. When he saw Charley, he stopped and smiled.

"What a busy morning, huh?"

She nodded. "It's been a while since it's been this hectic."

"At least we'll have plenty to cover for the five o'clock news."

"True." Charley swung her legs to the floor and stood. "I've been meaning to ask, how are your eyes?"

He chuckled. "Fine."

"I really worried I'd gouged them out or something."

He leaned against the counter as he opened his can. "No, it's nothing that awful."

"I'm so sorry. I can't believe I hurt you like that."

He shrugged. "It's my own fault. I should have known to block."

She walked over to him. "So you're not angry with me?"

"Of course not."

She let out a heavy sigh. "Good. I'd hate to think we'd just become friends and I've upset you already."

He shook his head and playfully punched her shoulder. "Don't worry about it, Charley."

She smiled and turned toward the door. "Gotta go. Catch you later."

As she passed through the door, her spirits lifted. She'd actually carried on a normal conversation with him without stammering, and for once she hadn't harmed him in any way. Thanks to Damien, her luck was improving.

She walked by Amanda's desk. Her supervisor leaned her elbows on her desk, her fingers rubbing her forehead. Long waves of red hair blanketed her face like a shroud.

"Hey, are you okay?"

Amanda looked up and gave her a half smile, pushing the hair away from her face. "Yes. Just a little tired from this morning's rush. How are you?"

"I'm exhausted, too."

Amanda picked up a piece of paper and handed it to her. "Got another story, but it's not pressing news. I thought you might want to take a look at it."

"Sure. I'll handle it." She turned to leave.

"Charley?"

She glanced over her shoulder.

"You look different." She tilted her head to the side. "Did you get lucky with Max?"

Charley felt her face flush. "Actually, I'm not dating Max."

Amanda looked surprised. "Really?"

"Nope. I'm in love with my neighbor." She grinned, turned, and left Amanda gaping after her.

Charley sank into her chair and set the paper in front of her. When she started reading, two words made her pause. *GIO Products.* She frowned and leaned closer.

It looked as if the vice president of one of their competitors, Herbal Sensations, was buying up GIO stock. Charley's heartbeat quickened as her gaze flew over the typed words. Nothing made sense to her, so she'd have to do some poking around to see what was really going on. It looks as if she'd have to call . . . Liza Scapolli.

She let out a frustrated groan and pushed her fingers through her hair. Liza was Damien's ex-girlfriend! Could she carry on a civil conversation with the woman who'd broken his heart? And to think the woman betrayed him with Max, his best friend.

Charley turned to her computer and googled Herbal Sensations to find their phone number. From the dates mentioned in one of the Internet articles, it seemed the family company was incorporated not long after Liza and Damien split. Charley arched an eyebrow. Damien had called Liza a scheming woman. What were the odds she was up to more of the same?

Charley gritted her teeth, then picked up the phone and dialed the number. After two rings, a soft voice answered.

"May I speak to Liza Scapolli?" Charley asked.

"This is she."

"Hi, I'm Charlene Randall from Sacramento's Channel Nine News. We got a tip about the power struggle between Herbal Sensations and GIO Products. If it's all right with you, we'd like to interview you."

"Pardon me? What did you say your name was?"

"Charlene Randall with Sacramento's—"

The woman on the other end gasped. "Charley Randall?"

"Um, yes." Charley cleared her throat. "As I was saying, if it's all right with you, I'd like to send a reporter out—"

"Why can't you interview me yourself?"

"Uh, well, because I'm not a reporter. I'm the research producer. I just call to set up the interviews."

"What if I told you I won't talk to anyone but you?"

Her heart jumped to her throat. Liza must know about her and Damien; why else would Liza call her Charley, not Charlene, as she had introduced herself? In her professional life, Charley went by her given name, Charlene, except among her close coworkers.

"Well, Ms. Scapolli, the only way we could conduct the interview is with a reporter and camera man. I'd be willing to talk to you, but I can't do the interview without my other team members. Do you understand?"

"So you wouldn't mind meeting me a half hour before the interview?"

"No, not at all."

"Splendid. How about this afternoon, say 2:00?"

Charley glanced at the clock on the wall. It was 1:00. "That sounds fine. Where can I meet you?"

"How about Norman's Café on Twelfth Street? It's just up the street from my office."

"Good. I'll see you at 2:00."

♡Chapter Fifteen

The minutes ticked by in slow motion. Charley fidgeted in her chair and glanced at the clock again. She could only think of two reasons Liza Scapolli would want to speak with her, neither of which was good.

To keep her mind off Damien's ex-girlfriend, Charley got online to read more about GIO Products. The name Giovanni leapt off the page and made her pause. Any relation to Damien, perhaps?

She continued to read. When she came across the name of the president of the company, she gasped. Damien? It couldn't be! Why hadn't he told her?

Charley rubbed her forehead as she tried to remember the few times they'd talked about GIO Products. Maybe he just figured she already knew.

She sighed. Yes, that was it. He hadn't really lied to her; he just thought she knew. At least she hoped that was the case.

She picked up the phone and dialed GIO Products again, but asked to speak to the president of the company. Instead, the receptionist transferred her to the vice president, an older woman named Bella Giovanni.

Charley tried to set up an interview with her, but Bella said she let her son handle these things, and unfortunately, he was in a meeting. However, the woman was kind enough to take down her name and phone number.

As the time neared for Charley's interview with Liza, Charley's stomach twisted in knots. Finally, it was 1:30, and she drove to the café alone. Her crew would meet her at Herbal Sensations in half an hour. Her heart knocked an uneven rhythm, so she took deep breaths to calm herself. Ms. Scapolli probably just wanted to pin down the exact questions the news station would ask during their official interview. But then why did Liza ask her to repeat her name, and why did she call her Charley, not Charlene?

After finding a parking spot, Charley killed the engine and climbed out of her vehicle, clenching her hands. Three steps into the café, she stopped and looked around. Sitting at a table for two in the far corner of the room, a woman with long black hair and a swimsuit-model body raised her gaze and met Charley's. It had to be Liza Scapolli. The name fit the woman, who slowly stood.

Taking a deep breath, Charley straightened and walked toward her. "Liza Scapolli?"

The woman stood and smiled. "Charley Randall?"

Charley held out her hand. "Yes."

After a brief handshake, Liza slid back into her chair. "It's nice to meet you." She motioned to the empty chair. "Please have a seat. Would you like a drink?" Liza turned and waved at the waitress, who rushed to their table.

Charley sat down, clutching her purse to her stomach. "Um, sure. Ice water with lemon, please."

The waitress nodded and hurried off.

Charley cleared her throat. "Ms. Scapolli, how do you know me?"

The woman lifted a perfectly waxed eyebrow. "You don't know?"

"Well, I know who you are, but I didn't think you knew about—"

"You and Damien?" Liza finished.

Charley nodded.

Liza's sultry laugh floated through the air as she drew her finger around the rim of her glass of iced tea. "I make it my business to know what's going on in Damien's life."

Charley's breath caught in her throat. She tightened her grasp around the straps of her purse and swallowed. "Are you aware my reporter will be asking you questions about your involvement with GIO Products, and the reason you have been buying a competitor's stocks?"

Liza smiled sardonically even as she lifted the drink to her mouth and sipped. Her deep brown eyes kept Charley's attention, and Charley knew secrets lurked there.

Charley had a feeling that whether she wanted to or not, she was about to hear about Damien's past with Liza.

Damien strolled out of the elevator with a whistle on his lips. He tapped his fingers on the handle of his briefcase to the beat of the tune in his head—the same song he'd heard Charley sing the night he'd helped her fix dinner for Max. Love did crazy things to a man, and Damien had never been happier.

Running errands this morning had kept him away from the office, but at least now he knew Liza couldn't sink her fangs into his throat again, or into the necks of his shareholders.

The lobby wasn't as crowded this afternoon, and he nodded to a few employees as he walked down the hall. When he neared the receptionist's desk, she stretched her hand out, palm forward, and stopped him.

"Can you please hold?" she asked someone on the phone, then pressed a button. "Mr. Giovanni, your mother needs to see you as soon as possible."

He nodded. "I'll go right now." Still smiling, he hurried to his mother's office. He hadn't told her much about any of the women in his life, but he couldn't wait to tell her about the one he wanted to spend eternity with. His mother would love Charley and would welcome her with open arms.

He knocked twice at his mother's office before opening the door a crack and peeking his head inside. "Are you decent?"

His mother looked up. "Oh, Damieno, you're here." She placed a hand on her chest and sighed, worry etching the soft lines of her forehead.

He stepped in and closed the door. "Mother, what's wrong?"

She pushed away from the desk, stood, and walked to him. "I just don't know what to do."

He patted her shoulder. "What happened?"

"I think Lisa Scapolli is up to something different this time. A producer from Sacramento's Channel Nine News called this afternoon to make an appointment with me for an interview, but I told her you would handle it."

Panic swelled in his chest. "Handle what?"

"Somehow the media knows Liza is buying our stocks. I believe they want to see what she's up to, and I'm worried what that woman will say to reporters if given the chance."

Damien shook his head, then grasped his mother's hands to stop their trembling. "I'll keep the news station away from us, I promise."

"I'm not worried about that, dear. What frightens me is the very thought of that woman being interviewed by Channel Nine. If they called us, they've certainly called her."

"You're right," Damien said. "Do you remember the name of the person who called from the news station?"

She shrugged. "A sweet young woman. I think her name is Shirley Randolph or Shirley Raddon . . ." Bella scrunched her forehead and tapped her chin. Then she smiled. "No. The woman's name was Charlene Randall."

"Oh, no!" With no explanation to his mother, Damien rushed out of the room and ran toward his office. When he neared his secretary, he called, "Get me Herbal Sensations on the phone. I need to speak with Liza Scapolli. Immediately!"

He hurried into his office, slammed the door, and tossed his briefcase on the desk. *This can't be happening!* he thought in utter frustration. Just when he'd finally found a woman who could make him truly happy, he was on the brink of losing her just because his greedy ex couldn't let go.

Running his fingers through his hair, he paced the length of the room. When his speakerphone buzzed, he ran to his desk and grabbed the handset.

"Mr. Giovanni? I have Mr. Jacobs on the line."

Damien swallowed hard. "Mr. Jacobs, may I please speak with your associate, Liza Scapolli?"

The man on the other end of the line cleared his throat. "I'm sorry, Mr. Giovanni, but Ms. Scapolli has stepped out. She's doing an interview with Channel Nine as we speak."

Damien hung up and dialed Charley's office number. After five rings someone picked up, but he didn't recognize her voice.

"Is Charley in?"

"I'm sorry. She's out of the office. May I take a message?"

"Who's this, please?"

"Amanda."

He blew out a sigh. "Amanda, this is Damien Giovanni. We met at the Christmas party the other night."

"Yes, I remember. How can I help you?"

"I need to know where Charley is interviewing Liza Scapolli, the vice president of Herbal Sensations. It's very important I'm at that interview."

"Well, we usually like to interview each company separately—"

"Amanda, it's an emergency. Please, could you help me?"

"Well, all right, but only because I know you mean a lot to Charley. The interview will be held in front of Herbal Sensation's building, but Charley was going to meet Ms. Scapolli in person at Norman's Café first."

"What time?"

"Um, well, the interview should be starting right now."

"Thank you." Damien hung up and dashed out the door.

Charley narrowed her gaze at the woman across the table from her and arched an eyebrow. "Ms. Scapolli, is Damien aware you're stalking him?"

Liza tilted back her head and released a throaty laugh. When she met Charley's stare, Liza shook her head. "Honey, you don't know what you're talking about. 'Stalking' is not the correct word in this particular situation."

Charley rested her arms on the edge of the table and leaned forward. "Is it correct to assume, then, that you are trying to take over GIO Products, and that is why you've—as you've said—been keeping a close eye on him?"

The woman let out another laugh that made Charley want to

do the unchristian thing and reach across the table to slap her. Instead, she balled her hands into fists on her lap.

"Miss Randall, I believe you need to leave these kinds of questions to your reporter."

Charley scowled. "Then tell me why I'm here. Why did you want to meet with me in person?"

Liza shrugged. "I wanted to see what I was up against."

"Up against? What's that supposed to mean?"

The arrogant smile on Liza's face widened. "That means I'm seeing what obstacles are standing in Damien's way."

"Why would you care? Your relationship with him ended seven years ago."

"True, but I'd like to continue our business relationship."

Charley clenched her teeth. No matter what that woman called it, she still wanted Damien for herself, and Charley wasn't going to give up without a fight.

The waitress finally brought Charley's ice water, and she gulped it down, trying to cool her temper. Then she set her glass down on the table. "So, now that you've met me, what do you think?"

Liza leaned back in her chair and folded her arms. "What do I think? Honestly?"

"Of course."

Liza took a deep breath. "Well, I'm surprised Damien is attracted to someone like you. Although I think you're very sweet and you have a pleasant smile, the man I know wouldn't go out with such a modestly dressed woman, nor one so reserved."

Charley brought her hand up to the top button on her pink blouse and swallowed hard.

"Damien likes sophisticated, ambitious women," Liza continued. "You don't appear to be like that. And he doesn't usually go out with quirky women, at least not for very long. I've done a little checking up on you, and I've heard about your past relationships with men."

Charley nodded. "So you don't believe he'd go out with someone like me because I'm not like you?"

Liza flipped her hand in the air. "You could say that, I suppose. It's just hard to believe he'd settle for you."

"When he could have someone like you, right?" Charley finished.

Liza's haughty laughter sent chills down Charley's spine. Damien was right. This woman was malicious—and downright evil, she might add. If Charley hadn't represented Channel Nine at that moment, she'd have taken her outside to teach her a lesson in manners.

"Ms. Scapolli, thank you for your honesty. I'm sorry to have disappointed you." She took another gulp of ice water and then scooted away from the table. "But the truth is, I'm the woman with Damien right now, and I plan to keep it that way."

"Is that a warning, Miss Randall?"

Charley reached into her purse, pulled out a five-dollar bill, and tossed it on the table. "Take it however you'd like." She forced her best smile. "Now, would you mind if I follow you over to your office to meet my crew?"

"Not at all." Liza threw a ten-dollar bill next to the five and stood.

As the woman walked in front of her, Charley's blood boiled. Was she jealous of Liza Scapolli? After all, the woman was everything she wasn't—tall, shapely, and beautiful. Could Damien be happy with someone as plain and *quirky* as Charlene Randall?

When they walked out of the café, Liza turned to her. "Charley, I can see you have deep feelings for Damien, but I think I should warn you."

Charley glared at her.

"Damien goes through women like he does his socks. You seem like such a nice woman, and he'll only break your heart."

Charley stopped at her car. "Then why do you want him?"

"I told you. It's a business relationship."

"If you want him for just his company, why do you want to eliminate the competition?"

Liza folded her arms across her chest. "If you really knew Damien, you'd know." She shook her head. "Charley, he's a secretive man."

She lifted her chin. "I think you have him all wrong. He doesn't hide anything from me. He's my best friend."

One corner of the other woman's mouth turned upward. "I can promise you, he's hidden something from you. It's just his way."

Uncertainty shot through Charley's mind. *He didn't tell me he was president of GIO. Would he if I gave him another chance?* Come to think about it, last night they both had something they were going to confess, but Charley went first. Damien never did say anything about what he wanted to get off his chest, but maybe he'd forgotten. "I think we'd better get going, Ms. Scapolli, or we'll be late."

All the way to Herbal Sensations, Charley's temper simmered. Last night with Damien had been a dream come true. Now new doubts crept in, and she couldn't get them out of her head. What if she wasn't good enough for him? What if she didn't meet his expectations? He'd dated several women in the six months she'd known him, and they were all like Liza—tall, beautiful, and perfect.

Why hadn't he told her the truth about his job? He'd acted like he was just an employee of GIO Products, when in reality he was the president of the company. Liza Scapolli was right—he had kept something important from her. What other secrets was he hiding?

Charley gripped the steering wheel tighter. Why did she have to think this way? Damien had told Charley about Liza's scheming and cheating ways, not knowing Charley would ever have occasion to meet the woman. Why should she doubt Damien now? He had no reason to lie to her.

She wouldn't doubt him, she decided. Liza was the villain here, and she had no hold over Damien. By the time Charley arrived at Herbal Sensation's parking lot, she was chuckling at herself and smiling.

Her crew had set up and the reporter was ready to begin the interview, until Liza held up her hand and insisted on stopping to fix her makeup. Charley rolled her eyes.

After a few minutes, Charley asked, "Are you ready?"

Liza nodded.

"Now remember, this isn't live, so if there's something we ask that you feel is out of line, we can cut it out of the final version."

"Thank you, Miss Randall. I have done this before, you know."

"Okay." Charley clapped her hands and turned to move away, but Liza reached out and grasped her arm.

"I want you to listen really close to my interview. You might just learn something new." Liza winked, then stepped away with the reporter.

As the taping started and the reporter, Tamara, asked the first question, a bitter wind picked up. With her coat pulled tight around her, Charley leaned against a nearby tree and listened intently to Liza's answers. Apparently, Liza wanted to merge her company with GIO Products, but the owners of GIO were not complying with her wishes. The woman overdramatized

179

everything, and now her lips formed a pout.

Charley rolled her eyes.

Tamara went on. "Ms. Scapolli, why do you feel GIO Products should allow you to become their partner?"

Liza's gaze moved and rested on Charley.

Prickles ran up Charley's spine, and she had a feeling she wasn't going to like Liza's answer.

Liza smiled malevolently. "Because seven years ago, Damien Giovanni and I created the idea for Herbal Sensations. Now that he's the president of GIO Products, I thought I should bring Herbal Sensations back home, so to speak."

Charley sucked in a breath. Could this be the secret Liza hinted about?

"Ms. Scapolli," Tamara continued, "why would Mr. Giovanni let you take the ideas created between the two of you and start another company?"

Liza's focus remained on Charley. "Because after our divorce, it was my half of our assets."

Charley gasped, and she felt like she'd been punched. Tears swam in her eyes and a knot the size of Texas formed in her throat. *Divorced? No, it can't be true! Damien would have told me!* He had mentioned that Liza was his ex, but Charley had assumed he meant ex-girlfriend.

From the parking lot, the squealing of tires caught her attention, and she glanced over her shoulder. Damien's car jerked to a stop and the door flew open. The man she realized she didn't really know jumped out and looked at her.

Her stomach roiled and everything around her spun out of control.

Lord, please help me! Damien found himself praying. *Charley knows.*

Like a tidal wave, guilt flooded his soul. Why hadn't he told her? He'd known she wasn't anything like Liza, yet still he hadn't been completely up front with her.

Charley swayed against the tree, her hands holding her head. Damien rushed across the parking lot and up the slope of green grass to her. When he came near, she opened her eyes and met his stare. At the sight of her unnaturally pale face, his gut clenched.

"Go away," she whispered.

"Charley, we need to talk."

She closed her eyes and rested her head against the trunk of the tree. "Not now. I'm at work."

"Mi amore, let me take you to my car. You look like you're going to pass out."

"I'll be fine."

Her voice wavered, increasing the pain in his heart. "No, you're not."

She peeked at him and then glanced over her shoulder to where the interview went on. "You're making a scene," she said without looking at him.

He grasped her shoulders but she yanked away. Her body swayed again, and he wrapped his arms around her, holding her to his chest.

"Damien—"

"If you don't let me take you to my car, I'll cause a scene, and the camera will be on us instead of on the interview."

She brought her hands between their bodies and pressed against his chest. Her gaze rose to his, fire in her eyes.

"I don't want to talk to you right now."

"Why?"

"Because I need time to think about what I just found out."

Her big blue eyes, now red-rimmed and puffy, pled with him even as they filled with tears. "I'm also afraid if we talk right now, I'll say something I'll regret later."

He dropped his arms and stepped back. *Lord, don't let me lose her!* he prayed. Yet he knew no one could force her to trust him; that would be her own choice. "I'll give you some space. But know one thing, Charley. I love you. I love you so much more than I've loved any other woman." His voice cracked.

Charley began to sob, and Damien felt as if his insides were being shred with a dull knife. Not knowing what else to do, he turned and walked to his car, hoping her sweet voice would call him back. When she didn't say a word, he climbed in the car, closed the door, and started the engine. He glanced up the green hill to the tree, but Charley was gone.

With a heavy heart, Damien pulled out of the parking lot and drove away.

Chapter Sixteen ♡

Charley curled on the sofa, her knees pulled tight against her chest. Amanda had been generous enough to let her stay with her for a few days—a few lonely, soul-searching days. She either wanted to forget Damien or forgive him, but right now she could do neither. She said more prayers than she could count, asking the Lord to strengthen her.

At work, the time seemed to pass in slow motion, and when it was time to go home, Charley dragged herself to Amanda's apartment, where she lay on the couch and stared at the ceiling. After two days, she decided to take some time off work.

Damien hadn't tried to call her, and she hadn't been home since the day of Liza's interview. He did send flowers to Charley at the office with a card telling her he loved her.

But how could he love her when he couldn't even be honest with her? Why didn't he trust her enough to tell her the truth? She'd bared her soul to him and shown him her real self, and still he couldn't be sincere. Maybe he did love her in his own way, but it wasn't the way she wanted to be loved.

The first evening, when they arrived at Amanda's apartment, she confessed to Charley that she and her husband had separated three months before. Were all relationships doomed to end? No, Charley's religion had taught her differently. There was a God, and He loved His children and wanted to see them happy. He wanted His children to marry and raise families in the Church. He would help her to find someone who felt the way she did about marriage and family.

The second evening, Amanda came home from work and then went out with friends. Charley'd crashed on the sofa most of the day, wishing she could stop thinking about Damien. Why had she let him sweep her off her feet so easily? Did he only want one thing from her—the one thing she would not give to any man until she was married? She gritted her teeth. He'd been a player when she'd met him, and perhaps nothing had changed.

Charley wandered into the kitchen and opened the fridge. Nothing looked appetizing, not even the chocolate cake doughnuts with icing.

With a sigh, she closed the refrigerator door, then walked to the guest room where she'd been staying. She plopped down on the bed and glanced at the nightstand. She'd brought her journal from home, and it lay next to the lamp. She remembered the next part of the article:

Way Number 9: Great memories. When you're together, make it memorable. Create memories by taking pictures or writing in a journal.

Tears formed in Charley's eyes again. As much as she'd cried lately, it was a wonder she had any tears left.

She picked up the journal and flipped it open. She skimmed over the words she'd written the day she'd moved in and met Damien for the first time. He'd offered to help with the heavier objects, showing off by lifting more than the moving men could.

Trying not to grin at the memory, Charley bit her lip. She even remembered the gray shirt that clung to his muscles that day, and how she'd tried not to stare at him.

With her belongings inside the townhouse, the moving men left, but Damien offered to stay and help her unpack. Charley could tell he wanted a physical relationship, and she let him know he would *not* get it with her.

She turned to another page in her journal. This was the day Tim had broken up with her. He'd accused her of not being serious about their relationship. He also mentioned how he wanted to live a long life, and how staying with her would only mean dying early.

Charley let out a snort and rolled her eyes. He'd always been overdramatic.

On a different page was the night she was attacked on her front porch. While in Damien's arms after the incident, she'd felt completely safe and at peace, and she realized he'd make a good friend.

When had everything changed? When had she started thinking more about Damien than Max? A sob tore from her throat and she buried her face in the pillow. Why did falling in love have to hurt so much? Was finding a man and keeping him really worth it?

Charley straightened and sat cross-legged on the bed, then reached for a pen. Turning to the next empty page in the journal, she wrote Damien's lies by omission. She wrote about what Liza had said, and especially about what Damien had done and what he hadn't told her. The more she wrote the harder she cried, but the anguish in her heart finally began to lessen. By the time she finished the journal entry, she felt as if a great weight had been lifted from her shoulders.

She would move on with her life, just as she'd done after the other men. She'd give herself another month, and then if she felt like it, she'd get back to finding Mr. Perfect.

Even if there wasn't such a thing as perfect.

Damien sat at the conference table with the shareholders, discussing Liza Scapolli and Herbal Sensations. In the back of his mind, he thought about Charley and how he could win her trust.

Since Liza's interview with Channel Nine, he'd attended church with his mother and realized what he'd been missing all these years. He had always believed in God; he'd just stopped practicing his faith. He had prayed more since meeting Charley, and now he realized that he needed the Lord more than ever.

Every day, Damien waited for Charley to come home from work, but she didn't. Her townhouse had stood empty for almost two weeks now. He had sent her flowers at work, yet heard nothing at all. He'd do anything to get her back, even beg on his knees if he thought it would help. Yet knowing Charley, that probably wouldn't be the key to winning her heart.

It was his own fault Charley had been hurt. If he'd been honest with her from the start, none of this would have happened. In the beginning, he hadn't wanted to give her his heart. Women were all alike, he'd decided, and none of them could be trusted.

Now he knew differently. Charley was an exceptional woman. She had loved him without knowing the size of his bank account or his position with his company. Women like Charley didn't come along every day. But since she wouldn't speak to him, he knew the odds of getting her back were slim to none.

Why hadn't he treated her better? Why had he assumed she was like all the other women he'd dated? All those women were like his employees that he'd dismiss at the snap of his fingers and never think about again.

All of a sudden he knew what to do. While it wouldn't solve his problems with Charley, it would disentangle this mess with Liza. For the first time in days, Damien smiled.

He cleared his throat and drew the attention of the shareholders. "Ladies and gentlemen, I have a plan."

"Sign on the dotted line." Damien pushed the legal agreement across his desk. "Everything is just as you requested. You'll work under me and my mother as the assistant vice president of GIO Products."

Liza lifted her chin as she picked up the pen and signed her name. "You don't know how happy you've made me, Damien. It's going to be wonderful working with you again."

He forced a smile. "After I had time to think about it, your offer made sense. Herbal Sensations is a great company; it just needed the extra backing. Now that I've bought it from you and Dale, we'll be able to give it the push it needs to rise to the top once again."

He took the contract and set it to the side of his desk. "You know you're working under me and my mother. You'll still be able to manage Herbal Sensations as if it were your own, per your stipulations upon selling."

She reached over and squeezed his hand. "You made a wise decision, Damien. You won't regret it, I promise."

He slid his chair back and stood. "Would you like a tour of the offices, or would you like to see your office first?"

She laughed. "I'd like to see my office first, then have a tour of the building, as long as you'll be my guide."

"Of course." He stepped around his desk and led her to the door, then opened it and followed her through.

Just as his employees had promised, they greeted Liza with wide smiles and praise. When he opened the door to Liza's office and she got a glimpse of it, her eyes gleamed with greed. She had to test out her white leather swivel chair and even spin it around a few times. She slid the oak drawers in and out before standing again. Then she hurried over to Damien.

"Oh, this is wonderful. I still feel as if all of this is a dream."

He chuckled and leaned back against the wall, folding his arms across his chest. "No, it's not a dream. Reality will sink in soon, I promise."

She grasped his arm with both of her hands. "I'm ready for the tour now."

He peeled her hands away. "Liza, you're my employee now. This isn't allowed."

"You're right. I need to act professional in public."

"Exactly."

When they passed Damien's mother, who stood chatting with an employee, she smiled. "Liza, welcome to GIO Products."

Liza gave Bella Giovanni a quick hug. "Thank you. It's good to finally be here, working beside Damien again."

Inwardly, he boiled. He hoped his plan would work, and that soon Liza would be gone.

When the tour was over and she returned to her office, Damien hurried to his office to take some aspirin. Acting as if he liked that woman had given him a massive headache and taken every ounce of his strength.

Later, as Liza was leaving for the day, she poked her head in his office. "Hey, are you ready to go home?"

"No. I still have a lot of work to do."

"So I can't talk you into going out to dinner? I bet you're hungry."

"Sorry, Liza. Not tonight. I'm not hungry anyway."

She shrugged and left.

Liza's second day of work was pretty much the same. She always seemed to be looking for Damien, so he dodged her, hiding behind corners and even locking himself in the executive restroom for a while. By the end of the day, he was ready for bed.

The third day, he was called out of town for a meeting. On his way out the door, his mother gave him the okay sign with her finger and thumb. He'd catch Liza in the act if it was the last thing he did.

The afternoon meeting went quickly, allowing Damien to do what he'd wanted to do for a couple of days now. Across the street from his office building, he sat in a borrowed car to watch—and wait. Darkness had fallen an hour earlier, and the light in Liza's office was still on.

Damien lifted his binoculars in that direction. Within minutes, Liza slinked to the window to draw the blinds. He waited for her to leave the building, but when she didn't, he knew it was time to make his move.

He hurried into the building, almost grateful Liza hadn't changed a bit in seven years. The halls were quiet, so he took soft steps toward her office. Just before he reached it, his mother's office door opened and Bella peeked out.

"Ready?" she whispered.

He nodded. "Let's go get her."

She hooked her hand around his elbow and they sneaked

toward the room where the product formulas were kept. He placed his hand on the doorknob and turned, but it wouldn't budge. His mother grinned and held out a set of keys. Thank goodness she was thinking clearly.

He took them, slid the master into the keyhole, and turned until a soft click sounded. Then he looked at his mother. "Are you ready to see something unpleasant?"

His mother arched her eyebrows. "Getting rid of someone who has cheated our company and broken my son's heart will be extremely pleasant, I assure you."

Slowly, he pushed the door open a little wider and stuck his head inside. The lights were off except one—the flashlight Liza held in her mouth as she flipped pages with one hand and snapped pictures with her cell phone with the other.

Damien squared his shoulders and flung the door open wider. It hit the wall with an echoing boom, making Liza jump. Just at that moment, his mother flipped on the overhead lights. The small flashlight dropped from the scheming woman's mouth, falling on the open files.

"What do we have here, I wonder?" Damien asked as he walked toward Liza.

Her face paled. "Uh, nothing. I was just, um, just—"

"Organizing the files?" Bella supplied.

Damien shook his head. "Liza, I wouldn't have thought you the kind of employee who works late."

She forced a laugh. "But of course, Damieno. I'm just trying to get to know the new products." She shrugged. "What kind of employee would I be if I didn't know what the company did?"

"True, but—" he stopped in front of her and snatched her cell phone "—why are you taking pictures? If all you're trying to do is learn about our products, why take pictures?"

"And in the dark," his mother added.

"Oh, Liza, Liza, Liza. I take it you didn't read over your contract very thoroughly."

She scowled. "What are you talking about?"

"Page 4 section 3 states that if there is any suspicious conduct by you, the president of the company can dismiss you immediately." He lifted his chin in triumph. "Because I have my mother as a witness, and we both think you are acting suspiciously, it is within our rights to fire you. You are no longer an employee of GIO Products."

She gasped again. "How dare you! You set me up."

Damien laughed. "You're the one who broke into this room, because neither I nor my mother gave you a key." He held up her cell phone. "Not only that, but the pictures on this will prove our case if we decide to take you to court." He held out his hands, palms up. "This time, Liza, you can't lie your way out." He glanced at his mother. "Mom, will you please see that Liza is packed and out of the building in ten minutes?"

His mother beamed. "I'd be happy to."

Liza ranted and raved, threatening to sue him. He laughed and shook his head, knowing that this time, she held nothing over him.

Of course, only one thing could make him truly happy, but if he couldn't have that, at least he had his company.

♡ Chapter Seventeen

Charley dragged her feet as she walked to the break room. It was a typical Monday, and she'd barely kept up with the news reports. In addition, a big snowstorm had hit that morning, causing several serious traffic accidents, and she'd been on the phone trying to confirm whether or not anyone had been killed or injured.

She stretched her arms and rubbed her neck. Of course, taking several days off work had put her further behind, and she didn't even want to think about Christmas. The holiday was only a few days away and she still hadn't done any shopping.

Charley stood in front of the soda machine, debating between bottled water or juice. Then she glanced at the snack machine. She could get a candy bar, though she knew she'd just feel worse after eating it.

The door squeaked open and Charley looked up just as Max sauntered in, pushing his fingers through his blond hair. When he saw her, he stopped and his hand dropped to his side.

"Hey," he said with a smile.

"Hey, yourself."

He walked over to stand beside her. "So, what's your poison?"

"Haven't made up my mind."

He placed some coins in the slot and pushed the Coca-Cola button. "Man, after a morning like today, I need caffeine."

"Yeah, well, I don't have the energy to make up my mind."

A long moment of silence passed between them as she looked at the beverage options again.

Finally, Max nudged her arm with his. "Charley, I think we need to talk. Want to go out to my car? It'll be more private."

Her heart picked up rhythm. Did he want to talk about *them*— about why she hadn't been hitting on him lately, or causing him bodily harm?

"Um . . ."

"Please." Max grasped her hand. "I think you'll want to hear what I have to say."

She nodded, and together they walked out of the break room and out the front doors of the station. A cold wind hit them head on, so she took his arm and they ran to his car. He opened the passenger door for her, then walked around and climbed in the driver's seat.

Max started the car and turned the heater on full blast. Then he exhaled a heavy sigh and turned to face her. "First, I want to tell you I'm sorry."

She lifted an eyebrow. "Why would you be sorry?"

"Because I feel a little responsible for what's happened between you and Damien."

She gasped. "What do you know about Damien and me?"

"Not a lot, but Amanda mentioned you and Damien were, well, getting closer, and after I saw the interview Tamara did with Liza Scapolli the other day, I realized what must have happened."

He took a deep breath. "Did Damien ever tell you about our college days?"

"A little."

"We were best friends and nothing could come between us, or so I thought. We managed to get through a few years of college before Liza entered our lives. She sank her claws into Damien the moment she found out his father was the owner of GIO Products."

Max rubbed his jaw and shifted in his seat. "I don't know how she suckered him into marriage, but they married in secret. I think they ran off to Vegas for the weekend. Anyway, Damien told me he didn't want anyone to know right away. I think he suspected she wasn't being honest with him. But I could also see he'd fallen for her. Damien never chased after women like I did."

Max took hold of Charley's cold hands. "She hurt him really bad. Did Damien ever tell you she cheated on him?"

"Yes."

"Did he tell you who the man was he caught her with?"

She glanced at their clasped hands. "Yes. It was you."

"Well, because of that, Damien hardened his heart. No matter how much I tried to apologize, he wouldn't listen. He quickly divorced Liza and dropped out of college. By this time his father was dying, so Damien took over running the company."

Charley blinked away her tears and met Max's stare. "Why are you telling me this?"

"Because I can see you're in love with Damien, and at the Christmas party, I wondered if he wasn't in love with you, too." Max laughed and squeezed her hand. "I also believe Damien was the one who sabotaged our dinner. I remember the cinnamon chicken recipe was one of his favorites. He made it for you that night, didn't he?"

She nodded.

"Well, I think he was the one who purposely replaced the cinnamon with chili powder." He shook his head. "But it doesn't matter, because after that, I realized he did love you. He didn't like the idea of another man being in your life, and he was around you a lot more than I was. Because I know what he's gone through— what Liza and I put him through—I understand his pain. I also know how hard it is for him to trust somebody."

"I don't understand," Charley said.

"I'm saying you shouldn't blame him for not fully trusting you. Although you're nothing like Liza, I'm sure it was still difficult for Damien to admit he loved you."

"How do you know he said he loved me?"

"I read the card attached to the flowers," Max said. "I probably shouldn't have, but I came by to talk to you and you weren't there, and I was curious as to who'd sent you flowers."

Charley swallowed. "He didn't tell me he was the president of the company. He didn't even tell me he'd married Liza."

"I don't believe he thought of Liza in that respect. To him, Liza was just a mistake he'd made, since the marriage lasted only a few months. And since it was kept a secret—" Max sighed. "But that doesn't matter. What matters is you can't hate him for not being fully honest with you. People he's loved before have hurt him, and it's his first reaction to harden his heart. He's also used to women wanting him because of his wealth."

A tear slid down Charley's cheek, but she didn't bother wiping it away. "Max, does Damien know how much you still care about him?"

He laughed. "No, and don't tell him. I deserved what I got back then. But Damien deserves a second chance from the woman he loves—you. Liza is very malicious, and she wants to break you and Damien up. By refusing to talk to him, you're letting her win. Do you want her to win?"

"Absolutely not. I can't stand that woman."

"Good. Then do something about it. Go tell Damien you love him and that you forgive him for not telling you about his past. Give him the chance to love you like he's never loved before."

Now tears ran down her cheeks, and she covered her face with her hands. Sobs tore from her throat, shaking her whole body.

Max's arms moved around her shoulders and he pulled her close. He couldn't know how much she wanted to run to Damien and forgive him for everything.

"Will you do that, Charley?"

She lifted her head and looked at Max through blurry eyes. "Are you sure he wants me? When he's had all those women to choose from, why would he pick someone like me?"

Max shook his head. "Charley, why wouldn't he want you? You're everything Liza isn't. You're kind, loving, and caring, and you're the funniest person I know."

She snorted a laugh. "Then you need to get out more often."

He laughed. "I'm being serious." He dried her cheeks again. "Please, Charley. Give Damien another chance. I know he'll make you happy."

She nodded and pulled away. "Okay, I'll go talk to him."

"That's my girl."

She took hold of his hands and squeezed. "And what about you? Are you going to talk to him and fix your friendship?"

Max sank back in his seat, gripped the steering wheel, and blew out a deep breath. "That's going to be harder, I think. I betrayed his trust. I was an idiot who'd been taken in by a beautiful woman." He shook his head. "Fixing our friendship will take a little longer."

Charley placed her hand on his arm. "If you'd like, I could put in a good word for you."

"You'd do that?" Max said.

"Of course. Look what you've done for me."

Large flakes of snow floated down from the sky as Damien stood at the window and watched the white stuff blanket the land. Inside his cabin in the Colorado mountains, a fire burned low in the fireplace. A snowstorm had hit hard the night before, and he was grateful he'd made it to Colorado before it started. Christmastime was always better away from the craziness of the big city, and for a man who loved to ski, his cabin retreat was perfect.

About an hour ago, he'd ventured outside to plow some of the snow from the driveway and road leading to his cabin. Then he realized he didn't need to bother, since he was the only person there and wasn't expecting anyone else. His mother and his sister, Michelle, were safe at home.

He'd given all his employees a week off with pay for the holiday, and he didn't have a single worry. But he did have one constant ache in his heart.

Charley.

Would the pain ever go away? She hadn't returned to her townhouse since the truth had come out. He'd waited to hear from her, and when she didn't call, he decided to give things one last chance. He'd driven by her work two days before, but saw something that caused his heart to break all over again.

In Channel Nine's parking lot, sitting in Max's car, Charley and his former friend were embracing. That told Damien everything he needed to know. It felt like a knife in the chest, a knife that kept twisting and twisting. She wasn't going to be a part of his life; she was with Max.

Damien's relationship with Charley been short and very sweet. And unforgettable.

He'd eventually get over her—maybe in a year or two—and be on his way to finding another woman. Yet he knew no one could replace her. He'd been through hundreds of women before finding Charley, and none had come close to having Charley's spontaneous charm and wit. None had made him smile so much. None had captured his heart the way Charley had, or made him feel so complete. None except Charley had made him think of eternal marriage and a family, and he wanted that so much with Charley.

Releasing a heavy sigh, Damien turned away from the window and walked to the fireplace. The embers popped and a mostly burned log broke in half. He took the poker and stirred the fire, then threw on another log.

Christmas songs played low and soft from the stereo, where he had connected his mp3 player. Though the songs soothed Damien's nerves, they also brought a deep longing that wouldn't leave. He'd never been alone during this time of year. Of course, the women who'd kept him company didn't really mean anything, but at least they'd kept him from the kind of loneliness that reached into his soul and ripped it into tiny pieces.

He moved to the heavily cushioned chair and sank into it. He stared into the fire, but only saw one thing—Charley's smiling face. In the image he saw, she reached out for him, her mouth forming the words "I love you."

A knot tightened in his throat and brought tears to his eyes. "I love you, too, mi amore."

When he leaned his head back and closed his eyes, he saw a different picture. Her eyes were puffy and red. Her beautiful complexion had turned a chalky white, and pain was etched at the corner of her eyes and around her lips. She pushed him away and told him she needed space. She told him to leave.

The song on the radio ended and another started, reminding him again how lonely Christmas was without someone to love. Then a low buzz began and he glanced at the radio. This wasn't part of the song. The buzzing grew louder. It came from outside.

He jumped from his chair and rushed to the window. Through the falling flakes of snow, a light shone in the distance. He squinted, peering closer at the object. *A snowmobile.* Someone wearing bright red clothes drove the vehicle.

Damien's eyes must be playing tricks on him, since he wasn't expecting any visitors. Maybe someone was lost. He hurried to the door and flung it open to a blast of cold air.

The closer the snowmobile came, the more it looked like someone dressed as Santa Claus. Damien grinned and shook his head. The person definitely had the wrong cabin.

He waited by the door and watched as the gas-powered sleigh approached his porch. The rider stopped and killed the engine, then climbed off, lifting a big cloth bag and swinging it over his shoulder. The weight must have been heavier than the person could handle, because he stumbled backward. After regaining his balance, he stomped forward through the snow.

"Ho-ho-ho. Merry Christmas!" The merry voice was too high to be a man.

Damien narrowed his eyes "Are you lost?"

"Nope, not lost. Just late."

Then the person looked up at him. Familiar, big blue, eyes met his stare. When she smiled through the fake white beard, his heart leapt to his throat.

"Merry Christmas." Charley held out her hands. "Sorry it took so long to get here."

A laugh sprang from his mouth and in three steps he stood in front of her. He slid his arms around her middle and lifted her, crushing her padded body against him.

"Charley, you crazy nut. What are you doing out in the middle of nowhere?"

The bag dropped from her hand just before she threw her arms around his neck.

"I couldn't let another day go by without finishing the ten ways to win a man. I realized the reason we weren't together was because I hadn't tried the final way."

"And what way is that, mi amore?"

"Take me out of this cold weather and I'll tell you. I swear my rear end is frostbitten, and I don't think I have any fingers or toes left."

Damien quickly pulled her inside the cabin and shut the door behind them. Then he picked her up, walked across the room, and deposited her in front of the fireplace.

"Ah, yes." She stretched her gloved hands toward the fire. "This is more like it."

He lifted the red Santa hat off her head, and with it came the full beard. Her brown hair tumbled over her shoulders. He cupped her cold face, his thumbs rubbing her cheeks briskly. "Better?"

She smiled. "Much."

She yanked off her gloves and placed her hands over his. Pulling them from her face, she kissed his palms.

His heart raced and a thrill surged through him. *Am I dreaming?* he wondered. "How . . . how did you know where to find me?"

She met his eyes and winked. "Your mother told me how to get here. In fact, she and your sister, Michelle, will be joining us soon." She smiled. "Damien, I had to come tell you how much I love you. I've loved you since that night I was attacked, I think, but I definitely loved you when you helped me make that chicken dinner for Max."

A knot of emotion lodged in his throat. "What about Max?"

She shrugged. "What about him?"

"Aren't you with him?"

She snorted a laugh. "You must not have a very long memory." She shook her head. "You're the man I want, not him."

"But I saw you in his car and you were in his arms."

She crinkled her forehead. "When was that?"

"Two nights ago outside your office."

She smiled. "He was comforting me and explaining to me about his former college friend. He encouraged me to give you another chance. I happen to agree with him."

"Then you forgive me for not being fully honest with you?"

She arched an eyebrow. "Do you think I'd fly in from California and ride a couple of miles on a snowmobile in this frigid weather if I hadn't?" She squeezed his hands. "I love you, and I didn't want to go another day without letting you know."

He picked her up again and sat down on the couch, still holding her in his arms. She tilted her head back and her mouth met his. His heart came to life again, and a feeling of utter bliss filled his soul.

Finally, he pulled back and smiled at her. "I love you, too." He caressed her cheek. "Thank you for making my Christmas wonderful."

"Thank you for making my life wonderful."

Emotion gripped his heart. "Charley, I never want to lose you again. I was completely miserable with you gone, and that's not a good way to live."

She tilted her head. "So what do you want to do about it?"

"I want you to marry me, that's what I want to do about it."

Love shone in her eyes and she nodded. "That sounds like an excellent idea."

He bent his head and captured her lips again, and the kiss was slower, more meaningful.

This time, Charley pulled away first. She sighed and lay her head on Damien's chest. "So, what do you really think about that Internet article? Do you think it works? Did I win your heart?"

He ran his fingers through her hair, lifting her face to his. "Actually, my love, I won yours."

About the Author

Since Marie Higgins was a little girl playing Barbies with her sister, Stacey, she has loved the adventure of making up romantic stories. Marie was only 18 years old when she wrote her first skit, which won a Funniest Skit award. A little later in life, after she'd married and had children, Marie wrote Church roadshows that were judged Funniest and Best Written. From there, she branched out to write full-length novels based on her dreams. (Yes, she says, her dreams really are that silly, and she's like that in real life.)

Marie has been married for 25 years to a wonderful man. Together, they have three loving daughters and several beautiful grandchildren. Marie works full time for the state of Utah, where she has lived her entire life. Marie plans to keep writing, because the characters in her head won't shut up. But her husband smiles and pretends this is normal.

Winning Mr. Wrong is Marie's first LDS novel. She enjoys hearing from her readers and may be contacted at mariehiggins84302@yahoo.com. Please visit Marie's blog, mariehiggins84302.blogspot.com.